Perspec
on Educational
Practice
Around
the World

ALSO AVAILABLE FROM BLOOMSBURY

Challenging Perceptions in Primary Education Exploring Issues in Practice,
edited by Margaret Sangster
Developing Teacher Expertise Exploring Key Issues in Primary Practice, edited
by Margaret Sangster
Global Education Policy and International Development, edited by Antoni
Verger, Mario Novelli and Hülya Kosar Altinyelken
Key Questions in Education, John T. Smith
Transforming Schools, Miranda Jefferson and Michael Anderson

Perspectives on Educational Practice Around the World

Edited by
Sue Hammond and
Margaret Sangster

BLOOMSBURY ACADEMIC
LONDON • NEW YORK • OXFORD • NEW DELHI • SYDNEY

BLOOMSBURY ACADEMIC
Bloomsbury Publishing Plc
50 Bedford Square, London, WC1B 3DP, UK
1385 Broadway, New York, NY 10018, USA

BLOOMSBURY, BLOOMSBURY ACADEMIC and the Diana logo are trademarks of
Bloomsbury Publishing Plc

First published in Great Britain 2019

Cover design by Alice Marwick

A catalogue record for this book is available from the British Library.

A catalog record for this book is available from the Library of Congress.

ISBN: HB: 978-1-3500-7634-1
PB: 978-1-3500-7633-4
ePDF: 978-1-3500-7636-5
eBook: 978-1-3500-7635-8

Typeset by Newgen KnowledgeWorks Pvt. Ltd., Chennai, India
Printed and bound in Great Britain

To find out more about our authors and books visit www.bloomsbury.com
and sign up for our newsletters.

Thank you to the authors from across the world who have contributed to this book. All royalties from its sale will be used to support the work of UNICEF.
Sue and Margaret

A huge thank you to my husband, John, and sons, Matt and Simon, for their encouragement, love and endless patience, and to my wonderful granddaughter, Willow – may she always be excited about learning.
Sue

Contents

Part III   A meeting of minds 157

Contributors

Jenni Alisaari works in the Department of Teacher Education at the University of Turku, Finland. She teaches pre-service and in-service teachers on linguistically and culturally diverse education. Her main areas of interest include linguistically responsive teaching, advocating multilingualism, language learning and especially language learning by singing.

Karen Collett is a senior lecturer in the Education Studies Department at the University of the Western Cape in South Africa. She has taught in a number of primary and high schools in South Africa and Namibia and worked in school development interventions before entering higher education. She has an interest in school leadership development and school improvement with a particular interest in promoting teacher well-being and enhancing social justice pedagogy.

Maria Elsam is a senior lecturer at Canterbury Christ Church University, UK. She is the Programme Director for the BA part-time Primary Education Programme and is Primary Science Lead. She is a member of the Association of Science Educators and a Science, Technology, Engineering and Mathematics (STEM) Ambassador.

Yvonne S. Findlay lectures in education at the University of Southern Queensland, Australia. She has over forty years of experience in education in both the UK and Australia. Her career spans primary, secondary and tertiary education as a classroom teacher, school principal and education advisor. Yvonne has a particular interest in the Rights of the Child and how these are protected in domestic legislation.

Mona E. Flognfeldt is an associate professor of English language and language pedagogy at the Department of Primary and Secondary Education, Faculty of Education and International Studies at Oslo Metropolitan University, Norway. Her research focuses on the teaching of English in multilingual primary education, teacher cognition and learning, and sustainable vocabulary development.

Anikke Hagen is an associate professor in the Department of Early Childhood Education, Oslo Metropolitan University in Norway. Hagen worked as an academic coordinator to international programmes and has long experience of lecturing in physical education, diversity and internationalizations in Teacher Education. Her research focuses on how international experiences influence preschool students' teachers learning processes.

Sue Hammond is a senior lecturer in Primary Education, Canterbury Christ Church University, UK. She works closely with schools, and her research interests include education for social justice. Sue was a consultant in Malaysia and India and has taught students from across the globe. She was formerly a primary school teacher.

Leena Maria Heikkola is a postdoctoral researcher at the Center for Multilingualism in Society across the Lifespan at the University of Oslo, Norway. Previously, she has worked as a teacher in Finnish as a second language and as a university teacher for future teachers of Finnish. Her particular interests are second language acquisition and language impairments in neurological populations.

Simon Hoult is a principal lecturer at Canterbury Christ Church University, UK. He teaches across a range of undergraduate and masters programmes with a focus on international and intercultural education. Simon is the co-lead of the Curriculum, Language and Intercultural Research group and supervises doctoral students undertaking research in intercultural and international settings.

Hanan Jibril-Dabdoub is a training supervisor at the National Institute of Educational Training in Palestine. Jibril-Dabdoub is also the coordinator of a collaborative learning project between the Ministry of Labour and the Ministry of Education. Hanan worked as a teacher for fifteen years and was interested in using innovative methods of teaching.

Christudas Amala Lal is an associate professor of English in the University of Kerala in India. His special area of interest is English as a Second Language. He teaches undergraduate and postgraduate programmes in English, as well as being a language resource advisor in various government projects. He also supervises doctoral students.

Alison Leonard lectures at Canterbury Christ Church University, UK, and has tutored trainee teachers in schools. She taught geography in several government and independent secondary schools. Her particular interests are Development Education and Global Learning, geography education, Special Educational Needs and Diversity, links between schools in the global south and the global north, and academic writing.

Melanie B. Luckay is a senior lecturer in the Faculty of Education at the University of the Western Cape, South Africa. She is currently the teaching practice coordinator. Her research focus is in science education, learning environment research, technological literacy and technology education, and she links her research to teaching practice.

Jill Matthews was a senior lecturer in primary education at Canterbury Christ Church University, UK. She has secondary and primary teaching experience and has collaborated on several international projects. Her key areas of special interest are the role language plays in developing children's mathematical understanding, creating inclusive learning environments and education for social justice.

Oliver McGarr is head of the School of Education at the University of Limerick, Republic of Ireland. His research interests include the use of technology in education as well as the use of reflective practice in teacher education. He has published widely on the subject of reflective practice and its impact on trainee teachers.

Molly Metcalf took a teaching post in an international school in Qatar after qualifying as a primary teacher in the UK. She is interested in children's play as learning and has been a keen researcher in her own classroom.

Eva Michaelsen is an associate professor of Norwegian language and literature pedagogy at the Department of Primary and Secondary Education at Oslo Metropolitan University in Norway. She teaches on further education studies for teachers, and her research focuses on reading in different school contexts – from assessing reading skills to teachers' facilitating literary conversations in the classroom.

Maria Mifsud lectures in English Language Teaching methodology in the Faculty of Education at the University of Malta. She has worked in secondary and foreign language schools in Malta. She obtained her PhD from the University of Nottingham, UK. Her main interests are teacher and student motivation, communicative teaching and digital technologies in ELT.

Joy Mower is a senior lecturer at Canterbury Christ Church University, UK. She is currently the English language specialist for the Teacher Education Improvement Project in Palestine. Working collaboratively with universities in Gaza and the West Bank, this project is developing Palestinian teachers' pedagogical skills in line with curriculum changes in the Occupied Territories.

Baraka Mwiyoha taught biology in several Tanzanian Secondary schools before becoming Head of Science at DCT Mvumi Secondary School, Tanzania in 2014. His special interests include a tree planting project, which serves as a conservation model to his community. He currently coordinates British Council's Connecting Classrooms in the Mvumi area. He is also a keen member of the Scouting organization.

Mirna Nel is a member of the Optentia Research Focus Area, North-West University, South Africa. Her main area of research study is that of inclusive education in South African schools. She has authored and edited several books and chapters on inclusive education and learning support and recently published articles on early childhood inclusion in South Africa and social participation of learners with special education needs.

Vuyokazi Nomlomo is an associate professor in Language Education. She is the current Dean of the Faculty of Education at the University of the Western Cape, South Africa. Her research interest lies in language policy in education, early childhood literacy, sociolinguistics, teacher education and gender equality in education.

Sissel Tove Olsen is an associate professor in Social Studies at Oslo Metropolitan University in Norway. She has wide experience of managing student teacher experiences on international exchange programmes, including an Erasmus-sponsored project that involved researching teacher well-being and diversity. Her key interests are multiculturalism, diversity and early education.

Kirsten Palm is an associate professor of Norwegian language and language pedagogy at the Department of Primary and Secondary Education at Oslo Metropolitan University, Norway. Her research focuses on Norwegian as a second language, multilingual and multicultural primary education and second language assessment.

Tika Ram Pokhrel is an assistant professor at Kathmandu University School of Education in Nepal. He teaches graduate level students on pre-service teacher education programmes. He has supervised students in teaching practice and internship for more than a decade. One of his main areas of academic interest is experiential learning.

Andrea Ramos-Arias is an illustrator and a research fellow at Canterbury Christ Church University, UK. She obtained her PhD in Education in 2017, with a thesis focusing on how children understand their sense of identity when interacting with picture books.

Mas Norbany binti Abu Samah teaches in the Mathematics Department at the Institute of Teacher Education, Dato' Razali Ismail in Malaysia. Her main education interests are in effective ways of teaching mathematics and developing assessments that assist student learning. Her PhD research focused on assessment in mathematics. She was formerly a secondary school teacher and has taught Mathematics for more than twenty years.

Margaret Sangster was formerly a principal lecturer in Primary Education at Canterbury Christ Church University, UK. Margaret worked as an advisor to primary and middle schools, was a principal lecturer in primary mathematics, and held managerial positions in higher education. She acted as a mathematics consultant in Malaysia. She has authored several texts about teaching, particularly focusing on children's knowledge and enjoyment of mathematics.

Stephen Scoffham is a visiting reader in Sustainability and Education at Canterbury Christ Church University, UK, and the President of the Geographical Association (2018–19). Stephen has written widely on primary school geography and is the author/consultant for a number of school atlases. His research interests focus on the educational dimensions of creativity, cartography, sustainability and international understanding.

Clair Stevens is a senior lecturer in Early Years Education at Canterbury Christ Church University, UK. She has a keen interest in child development and the science of early childhood environments. She has worked on Early Years' projects in China since 2015, engaging staff and parents in meaningful conversations related to young children.

Hilde Tørnby is an assistant professor at Oslo Metropolitan University, Norway, where she teaches English in the primary education programmes at all levels. Her research and publications cover a wide range of topics from numeracy and reading to aesthetics. In addition to her work at the university, she is a visual artist.

Heli Vigren works in the Department of Teacher Education at the University of Turku, Finland. She teaches pre-service and in-service teachers on linguistically and culturally diverse education. Her main areas of interest include social justice and diversity in education, intercultural competence, and identity building for linguistically and culturally diverse students.

Ellen Warrington is a professor in the Education Department at Mount Mercy University, USA. She has a PhD in special education and teaches courses in special education. Prior to this, she taught special education in schools, including eighteen years at secondary level. Her passions are learning disabilities, ADHD and behaviour management.

Viv Wilson is a former principal lecturer in Education at Canterbury Christ Church University, UK. She has an interest in comparative and development education and has worked in Malaysia and Palestine on educational projects.

Lynne Wiltse is an associate professor at the University of Alberta in Canada where she teaches courses in language and literacy and children's literature. Previously, she taught in First Nations communities in British Columbia. Her research interests include children's literature, teaching for social justice, minority language education, sociocultural theory and teacher education.

Vanessa Young is a senior lecturer at Canterbury Christ Church University, UK. She previously taught in primary schools and worked as an education advisor. Her specialist curriculum area is music and arts. Vanessa has been an advisor to national advisory bodies, an external examiner and a consultant in Malaysia.

Preface

Perspectives on Educational Practice Around the World is written at a time of significant environmental and political change brought about by globalized economies, social disconnections and technological interconnections. These each exert an influence on education, on beliefs about nationhood and the 'other'. A central aim of the book is to challenge some of the barriers that separate humans in different parts of the globe and provide insights into the ways that education systems are organized and experienced in a range of international settings. It does so through a series of short chapters, based primarily on the contributors' personal and professional experiences, raising questions for debate and deliberation. As with the previous two books in the series, *Developing Teacher Expertise* and *Challenging Perceptions in Primary Education*, the chapters in this text provide succinct, thought-provoking information for the readers, but this time with an extensive international focus.

Children and students around the world have many similar educational needs. Although this is evident when observing education in different countries, either first hand or vicariously, cultural and ecological factors also impact on how education is perceived and enacted. From these contributions we can learn how others are catering for the future of their learners amidst the challenges of global power and resource distribution. This collection of articles from writers in education around the world offers a glimpse into areas of practice in other countries. They may not be the 'big picture' but more a practitioner's view of how things actually function. One of the strengths of this series of observations is that they are set in the context of theoretical and research viewpoints, enabling the reader to place the observations in a wider educational context as well as offering an opportunity to reflect on one's own experience.

The strategies of other education systems may or may not work in our own country's education system but they are worth consideration and possibly trying out or adapting. What will these articles offer you in reflecting on practices in your own country? Other people's practices can challenge our pedagogical beliefs and even alter our practice. Get ready to be challenged!

Introduction

Margaret Sangster

'The world is shrinking.' How many times have we heard that? Extensive global communication means that we are seeing and sharing knowledge and experiences far more than ever before. International education is big business. Students attend universities in other countries, teachers visit and work in different education systems. Consequently, there is a growing awareness of the way education operates in other countries. There is a desire that education should be an opportunity for all children and students. The aim of the United Nations (UN) was to 'Ensure that, by 2015, children everywhere, boys and girls alike, would be able to complete a full course of primary schooling' (UN, Target 2a, 2015). And quite rightly so.

We hear much about Trends in International Mathematics and Science Study (TIMSS, 2015) and Programme for International Student Assessment (PISA, 2016) international databases and league tables both of which have inbuilt commonalities through their testing regimes. In reality there are enormous variations in education around the world. Each country has its own national interests; each country has cultural and societal differences, even different economic needs. There are bound to be prevalent national philosophies which are promoted through teaching and the curriculum. Certainly there are different approaches to education: in some countries, it costs money to go to school while in others school is only compulsory for primary age children; in some countries, it is entirely about acquiring subject knowledge while in others there are strong social and cultural objectives. How can fair comparisons be made between countries with such cultural and political variations? And yet they are. Political agendas change national education systems in response to international test results, because of the belief, one assumes, that this will increase the country's economic global impact and accompanying social well-being.

But how autonomous should education between countries be? Is it right that all children in all countries should receive the same education? Put like that it seems to be an extreme view but is not that the way international comparisons are pushing us?

Government directives are often the first overt move in bringing about change in education. These tend to be followed by curriculum development, teacher training and re-training. Assurances of successful change are sought through testing pupils to note improvement. (Also, to ensure change is being carried out!) Most tests are based on knowledge acquisition because that is easy to assess. Interestingly, it has been challenging to raise overall standards significantly as there always seems to be a low-achieving tail in these assessment situations. Leaving the high-fliers to fly, how do teachers deal with this worrisome tail of low achievement?

I believe that the recognition that not all children are meeting expected standards has led to greater emphasis on a further stage of development; a realization that societal attitudes and individual needs have to be accommodated to make education meaningful to *all* children. This recognition of the need to cater for diversity is occupying current educational thinking in many countries and this is reflected in several of the articles contained in this book. The meeting of individual needs could be seen as the gatekeeper to accessing any kind of education. For example, what is the use of lessons if they are in a language you do not understand? How can you learn if you are hungry? How can you become educated if you are not at school? These are the kind of issues with which teachers and students around the world are faced. The chapters in this book raise such issues and consider how governments, teachers and students respond to them, how they strive to overcome these difficulties.

All education and educators have a philosophy. Fuller and Clarke (1994) describe two educationalist approaches which they call the 'policy mechanic' and the 'culturalist', both of whom believe they can make education *effective*.

The policy mechanics attempt to identify particular school inputs, including discrete teaching practices that raise student achievement. They seek universal remedies that can be manipulated by central agencies and assume that the same instructional materials and pedagogical practices hold constant meaning in the eyes of teachers and children across diverse cultural settings. In contrast, the classroom culturalists focus on the implicitly modelled norms exercised in the classroom and how children are socialized to accept particular rules of participation and authority, linguistic norms, orientations toward achievement, and conceptions of merit and status.

(Fuller and Clarke, 1994, Abstract)

The different philosophical approaches described by Fuller and Clarke indicate how contentious education can be. What is actually happening in education around the world? This question can be responded to on many levels. What is the country's Education Policy? What is the expected achievement of the children? How are they taught? How are they assessed? Is there a social expectation as well as an academic one? At what age does education start and what is expected of young children? To what extent does the system allow for inclusion of all children? I suspect questions such as these are endless when it comes to comparing education in different countries.

It is impossible to capture all but it is easy to be sweeping and superficial. What have we captured here? These chapters are like looking through a lighted window: although you see a little bit of how a family lives, you only gain a fractional view. The following chapters give glimpses of how education functions in other countries. Each chapter is a spotlight on an aspect of education written by a person involved in that country's education. Whether the author is a primary school teacher, a high school teacher, a student or a teacher of teachers, they all have a view on education.

As a collection, the most noticeable aspects are 'aspiration' and 'difficulties of implementation'. We mustn't lose the aspiration, either in government policy or in expectations of children and students' achievements and the endeavours of teachers to give each child opportunities to make the most of themselves.

As a reader what can we take from these chapters? Primarily, they afford a chance to examine a small part of education in another setting, to set it against or alongside one's own practice and beliefs. Often, reflecting on situations beyond our own we see our own practices in a different light, maybe question what we do, maybe change what we do, maybe just realize the positive aspects of our own situation and be grateful. You could say that the writers and the readers of this book form a global community of practice (with a passing reference to Wenger, 1998) in an endeavour to understand and learn from the educational practices of people in other countries.

A final thought before looking more closely at the content of the book. This quote is taken from Young's chapter on Confucius versus Socrates and is a brilliant message saying get out there and experience the World.

> It is natural to continue to live in the world in which one was born, but to exclude the others from thought is to will to remain intellectually insular … Staying home all the time may serve one's comfort, but it does not serve curiosity, humanity, nor, in the long run, truth.
>
> (Scharfstein et al., 1978, p. 127, cited in Sumsion, 1994)

Part I: A view from the inside

This section provides views from across the world about individual countries and existing structures for children's education. Each chapter raises questions about education policy and the beliefs that shape pedagogy or challenge how it is enacted. Areas explored include: historical influences, government policy and curricula, cultural variation and needs, the appropriateness of early education and student experience. The writers all live and work in education in the countries about which they are writing and therefore bring with them the authenticity of personal experience. They are familiar with national contexts and current practices, but also consider ways of looking at the future of education.

This chapter by Ramos-Arias on Venezuelan education explores how extreme poverty, a failing and faulty system, corruption and cultural trappings impact on pupils' educational journey through the Venezuelan state education system. Ramos-Arias asks what education is actually accomplishing in such a troubled system. While Venezuela faces great internal problems not only in education, the next authors take us to countries where the spotlight is placed on the appropriateness of sustaining an 'imported' education system. For years Great Britain has exported its education system. Originally, this was because it had an empire to run but even today teachers from Britain go abroad to teach. Though this may have the advantage of many countries adopting English as its second language, Metcalf challenges the suitability of continuing to use an English curriculum in other countries. Using the example of Qatar, she explores the positives of this adoption and the conflicts that have arisen.

From a different perspective, in the chapter by Lal and Hoult, consideration is given to the impact of English medium schools in Kerala, South India, where teachers and pupils all use the State's unofficial second language of English. The English language has a colonial history in India but is now used as a key dimension of intercultural and professional communication. Their chapter discusses the tensions and advantages arising from English language usage in schools in a country which is now totally independent.

Findlay brings us a description of how a government operates to structure education in the context of Australia. Findlay describes how this begins with legislation. In this case there are two layers, National legislation and State legislation. This can lead to variations in law as well as interpretation. Legislation is followed by curriculum implementation that can be 'measured' by assessing children. At the same time, Findlay compares this with the content of the Teachers' Standards that have been introduced in England. There are plenty of questions here about effectiveness and philosophical aims. This draws the reader nicely on to how a curriculum is structured. With the focus on one subject, primary mathematics, Norbany binti Abu Samah explains how Malaysia is responding to an emerging world economy. In revising the mathematics curriculum the Malaysian Government is keen to develop human capital and creative, open-minded students. How often do governments indicate they wish to nurture the spirit of the nation? Maybe more policies should consider developing the well-being of students through the delivery of the curriculum.

Beyond a basic knowledge and skill-based curriculum is the need to ensure all children and students have access to learning. Most teachers are very aware that there are a significant number of children who find this very difficult for various reasons. The following collection of articles shows how some educators are endeavouring to meet these needs. Warrington takes us to the United States of America to describe the implementation of a policy called 'Universal Design for Living', targeted at support for children with disabilities.

Over the border in Canada, Wiltse describes how a collaborative University–Schools project is working to promote the education of an indigenous population through a social and cultural approach. As the world population moves through enforced displacement, economic imperatives or dreadful conflict, there is an enormous impact on the number of sectors of society who feel disempowered. It is crucial that education provides equal opportunities for all its children. This research links strongly with the article contributed by Alisaari, Vigren and Heikkola who consider strategies for helping children for whom Finnish is not their first language. They argue for a 'linguistically responsive pedagogy' and write about how this is being promoted in Finland. This article highlights the growing realization that curricula and teaching needs to be responsive to individual learner needs if children are to succeed in education.

Mifsud teaches English to students in Malta. She has observed there can be a lack of motivational synergy between students and teachers in this subject, so sets out to explore the relationship through empirical research. Along the way, she introduces us to the intriguing terms 'motivation web' and 'synergistic cycle'. This is a worthwhile and informative research study of benefit to language teachers everywhere.

To what extent does a government-led system impact on society? Hammond explores how these legal structures may have increased the divisions in society and brought about greater social inequality. She asks whether procedures aimed at raising 'standards' actually further disadvantage young children from low-income families. Has this become a form of social exclusion? We continue to visit early years' education, but this time in Norway. Flognfeldt, Michaelsen and Palm begin with a brief introduction to primary school in Norway as it is now and when the school-starting age transitioned from seven to six years of age. They question whether discourses about play, learning and freedom are possibly at odds with the drive towards more testing, competition and instrumental learning. They also discuss the tension between monolingualism and multilingualism.

Teacher education is a vital part of the education system of any country. This involves university and college tutors as well as mentors in schools. Pokhrel from Nepal takes us through the opportunities and challenges in collaborative teaching practice: creating milestones for transforming education and society in Nepal. It is always interesting to read how other countries train their teachers. This is a country keen to move forward economically and socially. With a new government initiative in 2017, the country looks to strengthen its education system. This involves the training of teachers and here Pokhrel describes the models used for training students in Nepal.

We now travel to Africa, via England. First, Leonard's account of four Tanzanian teachers' transformative experience brought about by a visit to an English university and English schools. They found much which was familiar in practices and challenges. The visit flagged up their own challenges and how they might use things they had observed to meet them. Mwiyoha (assisted by Leonard) continues these themes in the following chapter when he reflects on how the specific individual needs of visually impaired children struggle to be met in Tanzania. And then Nomlomo and Luckay describe how teacher training is working to meet the challenges of present-day education in South Africa.

There are many starting points and challenges along the way for education in all countries. The chapters in this section clearly reflect the sharing of practice and the desire to improve access to education for all children and students.

Part II: A view from the outside looking in

When we are inside a system we often accept that the procedures and experiences are familiar, similar to others in the system. In some ways a country's education system is a 'community of practice' (Wenger, 1998). To step outside that system and observe or partake in another country's education system will raise various issues. There will be the familiar, maybe strange practices, certainly unfamiliar environments and occasionally different cultures and philosophies. The chapters in Part II are a collection of writing by people who have experienced an aspect of education in a country other than their own.

Young explores the implications of two very different philosophical approaches to education – Socratic and Confucian that, it has been argued, underpin some 'Eastern' and 'Western' education systems. Using Malaysia and England as contexts, she explores how a 'Confucian' view contrasts with a 'Socratic' one and what lessons 'the West' can learn from a Confucian approach.

While earlier in the book Leonard discussed the impressions of four Tanzanian teachers when they visited Canterbury Christ Church University and surrounding schools, now Tørnby describes her visit to England as a 'transformative' experience. She goes on to explore the nature of transformation and its effect on her professional life.

Increasingly, students training to teach are receiving the opportunity to be placed in a school abroad as part of their training. Collett explains how Norwegian students have been supported to help them manage their placement in South Africa. Then Olsen and Hagen report on the Norwegian students' perceptions of how they managed in the South African schools. The two chapters consider the possible emotional impacts on the students as they negotiate a South African schooling environment that requires them to engage with cultural and linguistic diversity and inclusion. Collett highlights the role of a teacher well-being course in supporting resilience in challenging contexts, while Olsen and Hagen explore the notions of transfer and translation: processes which are relevant to all learning situations, wherever you are in the world.

Moving the focus from teachers and students to children, the following two chapters offer serious challenges to our thinking about the world we live in today. Matthews took on the challenge of working with refugees who had travelled from the war-torn Middle East and made it to Greece. From being a persecuted minority the refugees found themselves in a makeshift camp. Matthews describes how, with limited resources, the team worked to overcome distrust and chaos, to persuade children back into an educational setting, if a somewhat basic setting. This chapter captures a small part of what it must be like to be a displaced person with no means of support.

Scoffham takes on one of the big issues the world faces. With the global movement of people there comes an increased awareness of inequality, other nationalities and other cultures. Many children now live in multicultural societies. While this can bring great benefits and understanding, it can also bring problems. Scoffham suggests that schools need to play a key role in helping children form more inclusive images and develop intercultural understanding. This chapter draws on research findings to draw attention to this emotionally 'hot' topic.

Part III: A meeting of minds

The writers in Part I and II have viewed aspects of educational practice from inside and outside their systems. Through a mixture of conversation, interview and questioning, this section explores educational issues in a range of countries. It raises questions about the influence of politics, policy, cultures and the needs of the children themselves.

As colleges and universities around the globe encourage exchanges of students within courses, McGarr from the Republic of Ireland asks how module credits and placement expectations can be aligned both nationally and internationally. He also argues for wider access to international placements; something which may be challenging in a pervasive culture of performativity, where teaching competence is regarded as a narrow set of pedagogical competencies. Plenty to argue here!

While McGarr considers what should be credited, Nel and Wilson focus on the difficulty of ensuring education is accessible to all children in a post-apartheid South Africa. With at least eleven languages and innumerable traditions and wide cultural differences, this is not an easy challenge. This chapter links with many previous chapters where writers discuss the challenges of including all children in classrooms where there are children from many diverse cultural backgrounds in addition to having a range of academic learning needs.

One cannot underestimate the importance of education in Palestine. As an occupied territory it has little opportunity to develop tangible resources. Results in international tests have consistently been weak and prompted curriculum change. Elsam, Mower and Jibril-Dabdoub discuss what this means for teachers, how it affects how they view what and how they teach. What are the perceived tensions between policy and practice? This chapter reflects on how teachers have shown resilience in the light of change in an already challenging environment.

From Palestine to India: Lal and Hoult draw upon their experiences of organizing a series of study visits for UK-based student teachers to Kerala, South India. They examine their reflections on these experiences, considering how both Indian and English students were positioned and how this changed through these engagements. They illustrate their thoughts with students' reflections about their learning, particularly focusing on interactions with Indian and UK peers during a university-based conference in Kerala.

Stevens has experienced Early Years education both in England and in China. Here are her reflections on establishing outdoor schools in China and consideration of the positives and negatives of practice in both countries. She makes us aware that our own learning while teaching in another country can be truly life enhancing.

The penultimate chapter is contributed by Scoffham who, in an interview with Sangster, takes on the global issue of 'sustainability', an issue vital to every teacher and student in every classroom. He provides an overview of one of the key challenges facing humanity in the twenty-first century – how we can learn to live within planetary limits. He argues that sustainability matters because it is multidimensional, it is hard to define, and it is urgent. He raises pertinent questions about how best to introduce sustainability in classroom settings and the challenges of negotiating an area of learning where there is no set body of knowledge and where progression and assessment are highly problematic. There could not be an issue more important to humanity in the coming years, and as Scoffham points out, one that needs to be addressed with children as well as adults.

In the final chapter, Hammond brings together some of the recurring themes that have resonated with the contributors. She reflects on the issues concerning educators across the globe and then synthesizes the suggestions they make for addressing these. The solutions are not definitive, educating students for an unknown world cannot be treated simplistically or with absolute certainty. Indeed, there are big issues that education alone cannot solve, but the authors do urge that all solutions need to be based on equity and social justice, on cooperation, not competition for finite resources.

Throughout this book there is an underlying message of a desire to improve children's opportunities through access to education – in whatever form it takes. Whether this is seen as 'borrowing' from practices in other countries or reflecting and changing one's own practice through the knowledge gained from seeing others at work, it is truly aspirational. There is a sense of how important it is that, despite economic needs, we take care of our world and it is important that children are taught to know and wish to do this not only now but in the future when they are adults. There is also a sense that technology can help teachers, and children, to access their needs. Teaching evolves. It may evolve slowly but gradually current needs are absorbed and met. What will the world's future be like and what is the kind of education which will enable children, students and teachers find their way in it? Will internationalism predominate or will each country and society develop its own style of educating the children who will inherit their world?

Further reading

Fuller, B., and Clarke, P. (1994) 'In Raising School Effects While Ignoring Culture? Local Conditions and the Influence of Classroom Tools, Rules, and Pedagogy', *Review of Educational Research*, March 1994.

PIRLS (2016) International Database Available at: https://timssandpirls.bc.edu/pirls2016/international-database/index.html (Accessed May 2018).

PISA (Programme for International Assessment) Available at: http://www.oecd.org/pisa/ (Accessed July 2018).

Sumsion, J. (1994) 'An Exploration of Eastern Philosophy: Enhancing Understanding of Reflection' a paper presented at the *Annual Conference of the Australian Association and a key component for Research in Education*, Newcastle: Institute of Early Childhood, Macquarie, November 1994.

TIMSS (Trends in International Mathematics and Science Study) (2015) Available at: timss2015.org/ (Accessed May 2018).

United Nations (UN) (2015) http://www.un.org/millenniumgoals/education.shtml (Accessed April 2018).

Wenger, E. (1998) *Communities of Practice: Learning, Meaning and Identity*, Cambridge: Cambridge University Press.

Part I

A view from the inside

Part I introduces views from across the globe about specific issues within existing education structures. Although the papers are set in individual national contexts, they raise questions that extend beyond geographical boundaries and are likely to resonate with educationalists in various settings. They focus on education policy and curricula, research and practice and on the beliefs that shape pedagogy or challenge how it is enacted.

The issues include poverty and social inclusion, cultural variations and early education, at the heart of which is the quest for better and fairer ways of equipping students for the future. The authors provide ways of becoming familiar with a particular setting, its background and its practices, while also provoking debate about the universal future of education.

1

What is the purpose of education when an education system is infected by poverty, corruption and teacher shortages?

A consideration of the factors affecting the effectiveness of education in Venezuela

Andrea Ramos-Arias

In this chapter, I take an insider/outsider view to the education system in Venezuela. Insider/outsider because I stand at an awkward crossroads: I was educated in Venezuela to undergraduate level, but I have never been a professional in the field of education there. I left in 2011, and undertook further studies in the UK. Nowadays, education in the country has been deeply affected by political, economic and social unrest that puts into question the purpose of education at every level. Yet, these factors have only grown, thanks to a complex cultural framework marked by poverty, sexism, racism and homophobia, to which many in the country appear to be wilfully blind; a sense of dependency and cultural helplessness; and a marked tendency to pursue easy solutions (Barroso, 1998; Cabrujas, 1996; Uslar Pietri, 1986; Vargas, 2011).

Education and purpose: The context of Venezuelan education

In 1999, Hugo Chavez was elected president, beginning a new political era in the country, underpinned by a form of socialism he called '21st Century Socialism'. The Chavez era saw a string of reforms on every level, strongly railing against previous governments and publicly framing the opposition as being against the people. Chavez died in 2013, but his party has continued ruling through President Nicolas Maduro. Crime and social unrest increased steadily until 2013, but since, they have had a more dramatic increase (Herrera Nuñez, 2015). Poverty has increased in high numbers (UCAB, 2017) as the country's financial situation worsens daily, with the annual inflation rate reaching 13,779 per cent at the close of April 2018 (El Nacional, 2018).

According to policy documents dating to the Chavez government, education is a human right, conceived in a framework of building social democracy, rule of law and justice aimed at equality (Ministerio de Educacion y Deportes de Venezuela, 2004). However, the Survey of Living Conditions in Venezuela (ENCOVI), carried out by three of the country's leading universities (UCAB, 2017), gives a reliable, alternative picture of education indicators for the 2014–17 period. The survey indicates that of the total of three- to seventeen-year-old pupils who are enrolled, 88 per cent actually attend lessons and only 61 per cent report good attendance rates. Those who miss school report doing so due to shortages of food, running water, electricity, money to pay for transport fares or strikes. These affect over half of the poorest students, despite the government's famous implementation of education initiatives to promote education among the most disadvantaged.

What role does education play in a political and social system?

I interviewed Tucusito,[1] a head teacher at a private 'all-through' school, offering reception, primary and secondary education, and Ana[1], a nursing

---

1   All names are pseudonyms. Respondents were given the option of anonymity for safety reasons. The interviews were conducted in Spanish and translated by the author.

lecturer at a state post-18 military institution. Both educators have extensive experience in their respective educational fields. Tucusito has been a maths and physics teacher for over forty years, and her training was conducted in state institutions. Ana has been teaching medicine and nursing students for over twenty years, and trained almost exclusively in state institutions. Both women finished their training prior to the current political system. The focus of these conversations was to find what the purpose of education is in the complex framework that has been briefly outlined. (Their answers follow each of the questions in italics below.)

What is the purpose of education for your students, for the country and for government actors?

What are the purposes of education in Venezuela?

Tucusito: There seems to be a veiled purpose, felt in the policies approved since 2010. The educational experience has worsened considerably, both academically and in terms of values. I can think of four examples of this: young children must complete their reception education at a specific age even if they are unprepared for it, thus teachers encounter a very mixed bag of children with and without the maturity to be able to access Year 1. Secondly, most institutions do not have training or facilities to offer education for children with special educational needs, but these children are required to be integrated into mainstream classrooms with upwards of 30 pupils.

Following the above trend, these children are moved upwards through their education without necessarily being prepared for it. Third, secondary education has notably worsened, becoming less demanding for students and forcing teachers to continue to pass students even when they are not qualified. And finally, values of excellence in schools have been replaced with shortcuts, respect with mockery, and students fail to take responsibility for their actions. Until this [2017/18] academic year, the national curriculums for primary and secondary had not been revisited since before 1999, and they could not be found online or in print. Only this year a reform was introduced with no training or preparation for teachers.

Ana: The main actors of the current system used education as a system for national standardization, claiming that previous governments had not democratized education. In this way, many systems parallel to the existing state education systems were created through which the population can access higher education courses without the necessary qualifications. This led to students being able to 'complete' secondary education in a matter of months. About five to six years ago we began seeing the first cohorts of graduates from these parallel systems in various fields. I can only speak for graduates in health professions including medicine, but their preparation is far from ideal. Meanwhile, traditional state institutions are left in deplorable conditions: understaffed, under-attended, with fewer and fewer people training to teach. Physical structures are in a terrible condition without budgets for repairs or updates.

What factors do you think underlie the decisions behind a national approach to education?

In what way have the education systems and your students' performance been affected by the current national situation?

Ana: I would say it is twofold. Firstly, there are teachers with careers, political orientation and giving the response that the system expects from them as professionals. Teaching in general has become more difficult as more teachers abandon the profession or seek to emigrate, and those who remain face ever larger student groups, limited resources, poor pay that makes teaching an act of absolute vocation, the increasing physical danger of teaching with a growing criminality, and the deplorable state of buildings and hygiene. Additionally, and especially in government-run institutions, teachers are pressured to include political messages and to show clear political affiliation.

Then, secondly, you have students: most of the current cohorts were being born as this government came into power, and they don't know anything different. A year ago, higher education implied the possibility of a better life or perhaps even emigrating, but today students seem to not even be sure of why they are making the effort. Accessing education is fraught with barriers for young students, who must struggle with failing transport systems, the constant pursuit of scarce price-controlled food in supermarkets, lack of bank notes to make payments and the increase of violence. Students feel insecure and not committed to their education. I would describe our current students as very scared dreamers whose reasoning is clouded daily by concerns that their teachers largely did not know at their age, and this affects their performance, cognitive capacity, social behaviour and language greatly.

Tucusito: We need not wait for current students to graduate to see how their performance today affects their futures. Universities are already complaining about this, and have been for years: students arrive underprepared, with gross deficiencies in their subject knowledge and understanding across all subjects. For years, teachers have become scarce and this has been more marked in the last two, so students can finish secondary school without completing entire years of maths, sciences, etc.

Ana and Tucusito speak of how the present crisis in Venezuela is affecting education from every angle. How do their concerns relate to the stated purpose of education in Venezuela or compare to education in other countries?

How is your role as an educator affected by this?

Tucusito: Teachers are no longer leaders, they are not valued or respected by students or the Ministry for Education, their wages are miserable, teacher training colleges are nearly empty and there is no opportunity for professional development.

Ana: The way I approach teaching is different: there is no paper for making copies, students no longer have widespread access to technology or to the internet, and they have no budget for books or resources. There is more leniency in the formats and times accepted for submission of assignments, and the way they are taught to ensure they learn has to be very adaptable.

Ana and Tucusito relate changes in the perception of teachers and their approach to teaching as consequences of the social crisis. Can you identify factors in your context that affect teacher identity and role?

How can education help to improve the national situation? How could it help to resist, subvert, or fight the social and political status quo?

Tucusito: Many universities have developed proposals to improve education, but the government has not been interested in listening. There are also schools trying to resist the status quo but they are few, and their work can only be seen at an individual level. I don't think much can be done while we continue under this government; each one of us will have to do their best with their own students to help them along the way.

Ana: Honestly, I think that although I continue to be active teaching in my field, education is in such a crushing social crisis, without financial resources, adequate food, transport, books – I think it gives very little to this very disadvantaged sector of the population that we serve. I never tire of reminding them of the virtues of being a well-educated citizen, but for me there comes a point where my own discourse just rings hollow.

We see from their responses that the purpose that education serves goes beyond those stated in curriculum documents – there is also a hidden curriculum. What is the purpose of the hidden curriculum in the Venezuelan context? Can you find the equivalent in your context?

Further reading

Barroso, M. (1998) *Autoestima del venezolano*, Caracas: Editorial Galac.

Cabrujas, J. (1996) 'La viveza Criolla. Destreza, mínimo esfuerzo o sentido del humor', *La cultura del trabajo*, Caracas: Cátedra Fundación Sivensa-Ateneo de Caracas.

El Nacional (2018) *AN: Inflación de abril cerró en 80,1%* [online]. Available at: http://www.el-nacional.com/noticias/economia/inflacion-abril-cerro-801_233984 (Accessed May 2018).

Herrera Nuñez, E. (2015) *Evolución de la criminalidad en Venezuela (1990–2015)*, Caracas: Asamblea Nacional.

Ministerio de Educacion y Deportes de Venezuela (2004) *Politicas, programas y estrategias de la educacion venezolana*. Informe nacional de la Republica Bolivariana de Venezuela. Caracas: Ministerio de Educacion y Deportes de Venezuela.

UCAB (2017) *ENCOVI 2017* [online]. Available at: https://www.ucab.edu.ve/investigacion/centros-e-institutos-de-investigacion/encovi-2017/ (Accessed May 2018).

Uslar Pietri, A. (1986) *El mal de la viveza criolla*, Caracas: Cuadernos Lagoven.

Vargas, M. (2011) *País en regresión? Nuestras complejidades inconscientes en algunas imágenes sociológicas*, Caracas: Ediciones Centro Lyra.

2

How practical is it to implement national standards in an international setting?

The tension between conflicting expectations in the context of international schools in Qatar

Molly Metcalf

To teach in England, educators need a degree, Qualified Teacher Status and to pass a year as a Newly Qualified Teacher. The skills that are developed through these combined qualifications enable practitioners to acquire a good understanding of the National Curriculum, assessment procedures, and, ideally, a caring attitude to their students or young pupils. However, what skills and expectations are applicable when taken out of British schools and applied to international settings? This chapter aims to look at the education standards set by the British government, whether they match the criteria required by international agencies, and to question the suitability of the curriculum and expectations for children within the English system but being educated outside of England. It draws on the experiences of teachers working in international schools in Qatar.

In January 2018, the International School Consultancy found that there were five million students, 470,000 British teachers and 9,306 British International schools operating around the world with a British national orientation (ISC Research, 2018). This is a vast number of expatriates around the world applying the 2014 English National Curriculum (please note, the curriculum in England is different to that of Scotland, Wales and the Republic of Ireland). The expectations in British preparatory schools are, it seems, ever changing and increasingly demanding. Children are exposed to formal assessments from the age of three years in the form of entrance examinations and interviews, followed by formative assessments at age seven. While these are only indicative examples of the expectations, capturing just some of the assessment requirements, it is a concern that children in international settings may not receive the same instruction towards the National Curriculum (NC) goals as in other contexts where the English education system is implemented. Furthermore, there are many organizations set up to ensure that British education is delivered to the same standards in all corners of the globe, but there are likely to be cultural and contextual factors that affect this expectation.

What may impinge on the way a curriculum is realized or received in different international contexts?

In Qatar, British International Preparatory schools are expected to follow the guidance set by the Qatari Ministry of Education and the National Curriculum for England, as well as being endorsed by agencies such as The Council of British International Schools (COBIS). COBIS (2018) states that the organization 'provides accountability for the British schools abroad by working with the British Independent Schools Inspectorate (ISI), to accredit British schools all around the world'. This process is designed to help schools teach consistently and maintain conformity to the English National Curriculum (2014). To direct international schools and school development plans, COBIS has formulated five key aspects for British education based around the curriculum for England and its philosophy of teaching. These are as follows:

- Providing a broad, balanced curriculum
- Equipping students with the skills and qualifications to enter the UK system

- Offering a wide range of extra-curricular opportunities
- Giving strong welfare support
- Promoting understanding of British society (COBIS, 2018).

When teaching in any country or context, there are distinctive cultural principles and practices that permeate everyday life and must be respected, but are also dissimilar to the cultural mores in England where the curriculum has been conceived. These may be associated with language, family values and mores, or the local curriculum. Aligning these diverse influences presents challenges that can make the expected standards difficult to attain. In Qatar, the 2016 *Qatar National Curriculum Framework* (QNCF) is taught to the same extent as the English curriculum, although there are major differences within the documentation and guidance. For example, the English curriculum document states that science 'provides the foundations for understanding the world through the specific disciplines of biology, chemistry and physics' (DfE, 2014). In contrast, the Qatari curriculum requires that science 'focuses on the content essential for preparing students to be engaged and productive citizens' (Ministry of Education and Higher Education, 2016). In some ways they may be complementary, but there are also stark variations between the criteria.

What beliefs are implied in each of these? What principles underpin other curricula?

Another difference between the education system in Qatar in contrast to a British setting is that children are expected to learn Arabic and Islamic studies; this is for Qatari nationals too. This addition to the curriculum means that as well as having an extremely busy timetable children are expected to meet English curriculum standardized assessments alongside Qatari expectations. The Multiple Indicator Cluster Study in the State of Qatar (Ministry of Development Planning and Statistics, 2014) has shown significant differences between Qatari nationals and non-Qatari nationals. There are significant differences, for instance, between school readiness which is now viewed in a number of countries as an essential set of prerequisites for accessing formal education. Peckham (2017) defines school readiness as a culmination of social, emotional, cognitive and autonomy building competences that have been developed during the child's early years.

How appropriate, or desirable, is it to apply the same school readiness assessments to children in different parts of the world and in diverse societies?

Family values and upbringing vary across the world, but many educationalists regard it as important to celebrate the uniqueness of local cultures, their traditions, funds of knowledge and ways of being (see, e.g., Lynne Wiltse's chapter later in this volume). In contrast, the British government aims to introduce a Baseline Assessment in 2020 (Standards and Testing Agency, 2018), which will standardize expectations of school readiness. If this is applied in international schools, it is at risk of disregarding the distinctiveness of local learning. Currently, only 32.3 per cent of Qatari children attend early childhood education settings, as opposed to 45 per cent across Britain. Besides, just 77.3 per cent of Qatari children fit into the standard expected by school readiness measures used in English schools. To close this gap the British government could create a more flexible, contextual approach to international early years' education. Contrary to this, some may question whether it is the British government's responsibility to create a new contingency within the British curriculum for international use.

Should individual governments apply different rules to international schools using the English curriculum for teaching within their country?

Another concern is that we must give learners who have English as an Additional Language (EAL) an equal opportunity to access learning if they are to succeed (Grimmer, 2018). According to British Council statistics, there were more than a million learners with EAL in Britain in 2014. Therefore, a variety of resources have been developed and professional development courses are available for teachers. There seems, however, to be little support for British teachers in international settings to help children with EAL in their own country who are being educated in a British school system. With the school readiness rate being alarmingly low in Qatar alongside the struggles of EAL learning, there are concerns that children are starting school with multiple disadvantages. Penta International suggests that to be an outstanding British school in the state of Qatar the school will comply with the directives of the Supreme Education Council while delivering an essentially British educational learning experience. This is founded on the premise that the curriculum is broad and well balanced, promotes intellectual curiosity, independent learning and creativity (BSO Inspectorate by Penta International, 2017).

Who are the curriculum and specific pedagogy aimed at: local children receiving an educational in their home city, or expatriate international students having a British education abroad?

The aim of this chapter has not been to present a negative picture of teaching internationally, which has many rewards, but to provoke debate about possible conflicts in the enactment of national standards in international settings. When school readiness standards are found to be lower than expected in a British setting, it seems unrealistic to presume young children will be able to access the curriculum immediately, or progress at the same rate (or in the same perhaps monocultural way) as children in the country from which the curriculum originates. Although increasing the percentage of Qataris attending early childhood education could potentially close the gap between Qatari nationals and non-Qataris, applying English school readiness measures or the proposed Baseline Assessment could lead to other tensions. Children or older students in international schools following the statutory English National Curriculum (2014) cannot be isolated from the cultural expectations of the host community. Indeed, differences in culture and beliefs about the upbringing of children should be preserved. Yet, that does pose the question of whether the British education system is completely compatible in countries that are vastly divergent to Britain, or what impact these dissonances may have on the children and teachers involved in such institutions. Maybe it is time to consider the need for 'fluidity and provisionality in global societies' (Andreotti, 2010, p. 5), resisting the 'instrumentalist thinking' (2010, p. 9) that rigid perceptions of knowledge could impose.

Further reading

Andreotti, V. (2010) 'Global Education in the "21st Century": Two different Perspectives on the "Post-" of Postmodernism', *International Journal of Development Education and Global Learning* 2:2.

British Council (2014) Available at: https://www.britishcouncil.org/voices-magazine/how-uk-schools-support-young-learners-english (Accessed April 2018).

BSO Inspectorate by Penta International (2017) Available at: http://www.pentainternational.co.uk/BSO/Doha%20College,%20Qatar%20-%20 25.01.2015%20-%20final.pdf (Accessed April 2018).

COBIS (2018) Available at: https://www.cobis.org.uk/about-us/british-international-schools/why-a-british-education (Accessed April 2018).

Department for Education (2014) *National Curriculum in England: Framework for Key Stages 1 to 4*, London: Department for Education Available at: https://www.gov.uk/government/publications/

national-curriculum-in-england-framework-for-key-stages-1-to-4 (Accessed April 2018).

Department for Education, Standards and Testing Agency (2018) *Baseline Assessment*, Available at: https://www.gov.uk/guidance/reception-baseline-assessment (Accessed May 2018).

DfE (2011) Available at: https://assets.publishing.service.gov.uk/government/uploads/system/uploads/attachment_data/file/665520/Teachers__Standards.pdf (Accessed April 2018).

Grimmer, T. (2018) *School Readiness and the Characteristics of Effective Learning: The Essential Guide for Early Years Practitioners*, London: Jessica Kingsley Publishers.

ISC Research (January 2018) Retrieved from Independent, unrivalled market intelligence on the world's international schools available at: https://www.iscresearch.com (Accessed May 2018).

Ministry Of Development Planning and Statistics (2014) 'Multiple Indicator Cluster Survey (MICS): 2012 – the Situation of Children and Women', in *Multiple Indicator Cluster Survey (MICS)* available at: https://www.unicef.org/statistics/index_24302.html (Accessed May 2018).

Ministry of Education and Higher Education, Q. (2018) Available at: http://www.edu.gov.qa/En/SECInstitutes/EducationInstitute/Offices/Pages/ScienceStandards.aspx (Accessed April 2018).

Peckham, K. (2017) *Developing School Readiness: Creating Lifelong Learners*, London: SAGE.

Penta International: The British Schools Overseas (2017) Available at: http://www.pentainternational.co.uk/bso.php (Accessed May 2018).

3

An imperial relic or preparation for global society? What are the issues of having English-medium schools?

An examination of the influence of the continued use of English-medium teaching in southern India

Simon Hoult and Christudas Amala Lal

A fundamental dimension to English-medium schools is that the teaching and learning is almost entirely conducted using English, which we argue has a contentious colonial past, not least in Kerala, South India. Kerala is the focus of our discussion in this chapter about the issues of having English-medium schools. Despite such histories, to which we can add the contemporary neocolonial dimension to the English language through its global business use by transnational corporations, we argue there are other factors related to English-medium education that inhibit students' learning in the globalized era within which we live.

English is the Keralan state's unofficial second language and English-medium schools are a popular form of education. They were often associated with private schools, some of which draw a history from Christian missionary schools. Such schools, however, aim to be accessible to a wide range of parents and thus should not be associated with the economically elite private schools of the 'West'. In recent years the nature of English-medium schools has broadened in Kerala. Some of the major English-medium schools are managed by Christian denominations, largely Catholic, and the Christian missionary origins should not be overlooked. Nonetheless, Hindu and Muslim managements too have invested heavily in English-medium education throughout the State. There are some that are run by Hindu organizations, such as the Chinmaya Mission, Nair Service Society and Sree Narayana Dharma Paripalana Yogam and others by the Muslim educational agencies, including the Muslim Educational Society and the Muslim Association. Therefore, there is a range of religious groups running similar schools across Kerala.

The government is also a major investor in English-medium schools. With the threat of private schools taking away the lion's share of students, there has been a great increase in English-medium divisions in schools totally owned by the government. For example, in Thiruvananthapuram, the State capital, there is a government-owned school called Cotton Hill Girls High School, and a government-aided school, St. Mary's Higher Secondary School, managed by the Malankara Syrian Catholic denomination. According to Kerala Government information (2011), they are two of the largest schools in Asia, with respectively four thousand and twelve thousand students on role. Each school has considerable divisions set aside for students who have opted to do their studies in the English medium.

What do you think are the implications for students and teachers who learn and teach through a language that is, in almost all cases, not their first language?

The English language has a contentious and complex history in India, growing in status and use as a consequence of British colonialism and the associated 'civilization' and education of the Indian people (Viswanathan, 1987). Underneath the modern Indian Education system is a foundation built during British rule. Over 180 years ago Lord Macaulay, first Law Member of the Governor-General of India's Council, proposed a 'Western' education system beyond that of the existing 'Oriental education'. It included establishing English-medium universities and schools as Indian languages were 'incomplete, inefficient and lacking scientific vocabulary' (Sharma and Sharma, 2000, p. 81). In contrast, the English language was regarded as 'pre-eminent even amongst the languages of the West' (2000, p. 80).

Why do you think imperialists such as Macauley promoted such ideas so strongly about the need for an English-medium education in India?

It is easy to see how Imperialist views about colonized cultures resulted in the British Empire being seen as a 'cultural bomb' (Wa Thiong'o, 1986, p. 3) which, in India, devalued traditional and ancient educational philosophies and promoted Eurocentric philosophies through colonial educational reform (Sen, 2005). Wa Thiong'o (1986, p. 3) explains that colonialism disrupts the colonized people's

> *belief in their names, in their languages, in their environment, in their heritage of struggle, in their unity, in their capacities and ultimately in themselves. It makes them see their past as one wasteland of non-achievement and it makes them want to distance themselves from that wasteland.*

The use of English, especially in school, has thus created for many Keralites potential differences between what Bhabha (1994/2004, p. xx) terms the 'language lived' and the 'language learned', and the meaning of what it is 'to survive, to produce, to labor [*sic*] and to create, within a world-system whose major economic impulses and cultural investments are pointed in a direction away from you, your country or your people' (Bhabha 1994/2004). Such a tension is significant, as Wa Thiong'o (1986, p. 4) explains, 'the choice of language and the use to which language is put is central to a people's definition of themselves'. However, India now consists of 1.3 billion people with one of the world's largest economies. Indian English is a globally significant language and more than seventy years after independence it perhaps veers towards essentialism to claim that local cultures are totally suppressed as a result of the use of English. Additionally, students of all creeds attend English-medium schools in Kerala, which often emerge as centres of cultural sharing within the apparently homogenous geopolitical domain. This is particularly significant as even today the mutual exclusiveness in cultural practices within the state is very marked, particularly on the basis of caste and religion.

How might learning through the English medium make students feel about their first language? What might this imply about their local cultures?

It is arguably significant to consider the nature of pedagogy and the curriculum within Keralan education. Curriculum content and the process of teaching and learning may be significant dimensions that influence the way English medium is perceived and the extent to which local or Eurocentric cultures are privileged. The dominant pedagogy employed in many Keralan schools, described as 'teacher-orientated and non-participatory [and] encouraging learning by rote' (George, 2006, p. 279), arguably leads to a 'stifling of curiosity, creativity and initiative of students and teachers' (George, 2006). Such pedagogic approaches are reminiscent of traditional forms of British education prior to the introduction of more learner-centred approaches and it is, perhaps, this colonial relic that influences young Keralites more than the colonial heritage of the English language through which some are educated. Sen (2006) linked these outcomes to the problems of finding suitably skilled young people for a modern workforce that required application of knowledge and skills rather than just content knowledge. It is possibly one reason why Kerala's unrivalled social indicators in India are not matched by its economic ones, and this social advancement with limited economic development has become to signify the 'Kerala Experience' (McKibben, 1996). Maybe we should be arguing for greater and better use of English-medium schools so that the English language can be applied effectively in wider life, including employment, in order for places such as Kerala to make further economic advancement.

What are the pros and cons of this argument?

The colonial hangover that has favoured English above the local language of Malayalam has waned to a great extent in Kerala, yet the English language continues to have privileged status for other reasons. This is primarily attributable to the practical benefits of its mastery, such as employability, and often there is a strong tendency to rate English over the native language to the extent of creating a generation of students who live in cultural hybridity. English-medium schools have made attempts to keep the regional cultural values within the curriculum, however, often there still pervades a sense of colonial mimicry of the 'West' in this curriculum. This creates hindrances for young Indians to critique ideas of Eurocentric cultural privilege and for the path of English language education itself, which would benefit from a more communicative and learner-centred approach to its teaching. The prioritization of the English language and the attempt at the immersion pedagogic model, where subjects are all taught in a foreign language, do pose major problems to the quality of teaching. The persistent teacher centredness, and the continuing emphasis on overt teaching of grammatical rules in English language classes in the state, keep the application of the language learned minimal, preventing strong participating in, as well as critiquing, global society. It is imperative to review and revise the priorities of English-medium education, which would benefit largely if it could be freed from the restraints of a curriculum and pedagogic approach with colonial traces and mimicry of antiquated 'Western' approaches.

Why do you think pedagogic approaches and curriculum content still tend to mimic former colonialists' approaches to education?

In this short chapter we have argued that the English language in Kerala has a contentious colonial history. Moreover, its continued use as a means for young Indians to become global citizens has implications for the way they may privilege Eurocentric cultures. However, this is not through their use of the English language per se and rather the stifling of curiosity and criticality associated with developing independent young minds through a curriculum and pedagogy that mimics its colonial ancestors is a more crucial matter that requires urgent review.

Further reading

Adichie, C. (2009) *The Danger of a Single Story*, TED Lecture, July 2009, Available at: http://www.ted.com/talks/chimamanda_adichie_the_danger_of_a_single_story.html (Accessed 16 May 2013).

Bhabha, H. (1994/2004) *The Location of Culture*, Abingdon: Routledge.

George, K. (2006) 'Kerala's Education System: An Insider's View', in Tharamangalam, J. (ed.), *Kerala: The Paradoxes of Public Action and Development*, New Delhi: Orient Longman.

Kerala Government (2011) *List of High Schools in Thiruvananthapuram District*. Available at: http://education.kerala.gov.in/Downloads2011/Notifications/statitics/hs/tvm.pdf (Accessed July 2018).

Khilnani, S. (2003) *The Idea of India*, New Delhi: Penguin Books.

McKibben, B. (1996) 'The Enigma of Kerala: One State in India Is Proving the Development Experts Wrong', *Utne Reader*, March–April, pp. 103–12.

Sen, A. (2005) *The Argumentative Indian: Writings on Indian Culture, History and Identity*, London: Penguin Books.

Sen, A. (2006) 'Education in Kerala's Development: Towards a New Agenda', in Tharamangalam, J. (ed.), *Kerala: The Paradoxes of Public Action and Development*, New Delhi: Orient Longman, pp. 258–72.

Sharma, R., and Sharma, R. K. (2000) *History of Education in India*, New Delhi: Atlantic.

Viswanathan, G. (1987) *Masks of Conquest: Literary Study and British Rule in India*, London: Faber.

Wa Thiong'o, N. (1986) *Decolonising the Mind: The Politics of Language in African Literature*, Oxford: James Curry.

4

Who decides what should be taught in our schools and why?

The extent to which the curriculum is dictated by governing institutions in Australia

Yvonne S. Findlay

The policy matrix in Australia is complex. There are two main layers of legislature: the Federal Government which sits in Canberra (capital of Australia) and has two major and several minor parties based in two legislative houses, and then eight separate state parliaments that also make laws which govern their own state. This chapter explores some of the tensions arising from conflicting and, in some cases, non-implementation of policy.

The Federal Government has a national responsibility for education. A major policy document issued by the Federal Government is the 'Melbourne Declaration on Educational Goals for Young Australians' (MCEETYA, 2008). The declaration sets out the goals and objectives considered necessary to provide a twenty-first-century education for our children and young people to enable them to reach their full potential. Two principal goals were identified:

Australian schooling promotes equity and excellence. All young Australians become:

- successful learners
- confident and creative individuals
- active and informed citizens.

Among the plethora of policies emanating from the declaration three in particular have significant impact on schools and teachers. They are the Australian Curriculum, national testing and the development of standards for teachers.

The Australian Curriculum is administered by the Australian Curriculum Assessment and Reporting Authority (ACARA). Similar to such documents in other countries, the ACARA documents set out the curriculum content expected across all subject areas and cover all years of schooling from year one to year twelve. The title of Australian Curriculum rather than National Curriculum is important because this highlights a specific anomaly. Each state and territory exercises control over its own education provision and not all have agreed to fully implement the ACARA guidelines. The result of this is that the guidelines are adapted by individual states and territories and operationalized in each system to a greater or lesser degree. In a similar way to the countries of the United Kingdom, there is no single Australian education system. For example, in New South Wales (NSW), the prescribed curriculum does not follow the format of the Australian Curriculum. Rather, it sets out learning objectives as deemed appropriate by the state government. The NSW curriculum may parallel the Australian Curriculum but does not exactly adhere to every aspect of it.

What are the implications for potential conflict between state, state and Federal governments?

Another principal area of Australian school education nationally is the *National Assessment Programme Language and Numeracy* (NAPLAN). Within this, all students are required to take standardized tests during Years 3, 5, 7 and 9. The initial purpose of the tests was as a diagnostic tool to enable teachers to match classroom practice to meet the identified learning needs of the students. It has, however, morphed into a high-stakes test with individual school and class results published on the national 'My School' website. As a result, schools have become subject to scrutiny based only on their published NAPLAN results rather than the overall quality of the learning and teaching happening in the school across all curriculum areas. Neither is any account taken of the 'value-added' activities which create the social learning and inclusive aspects of the whole school community.

Explore the tension between diagnostic testing and external use of results. Is this true in other countries?

The requirements of the twenty-first-century workforce are different from those of the nineteenth and even the twentieth century, but school education remains the primary agent in preparing our young people to take their place in the world.

Do you think that the 'traditional' curriculum content and organization still evident in schools is appropriate to meet the learning needs of the twenty-first-century student?

Delors (1996, pp. 20–2) wrote *Learning: The Treasure Within* in which he identified four key guiding principles for twenty-first-century education: 'Learning to know', 'Learning to do', 'Learning to live together' and 'Learning to be'. An examination of these four key areas is a reminder that learning in the twenty-first century should go beyond the traditional curriculum of subject silos and should embrace the following:

- content knowledge and understanding;
- critical thinking abilities to enable the considered analysis and synthesis of information available through digital technologies;
- the skills to apply knowledge in new ways; the development of interpersonal skills to enable working with peers across continents and contexts; and
- intrapersonal skills to understand how each one of us has a place in the sometimes anonymized twenty-first-century digital world.

Do national testing regimes enable or hinder appropriate twenty-first-century learning?

The inevitable narrowing of the curriculum taught in classrooms to enable teachers and students to meet the requirements of the tests, could lead to the skills and attributes identified by Delors to be a secondary consideration. The predominant workplace culture may be that of the digital age but the testing regimes lock schooling into narrow, prescribed subject silos so that tests can be passed.

To what extent do other countries value Delors' principles?

A further example of government-led policy can be seen in the English education system where the revised Teachers' Standards (2011) stipulate that teachers uphold 'fundamental British values, including democracy, the rule of law, individual liberty and mutual respect and tolerance of those with different faiths and beliefs' (DfE, 2011, p. 10). This policy was introduced as a response to a sharp increase in immigration numbers during previous years. Its inclusion in the Teachers' Standards reflects the evolving sociocultural nature of the English population. However, such an inclusion assumes that the concept of 'fundamental British values' is commonly understood. The values of the current government are dominant in such a statement since it is the government of the day who dictate the teacher standards. There is no commonly delineated statement of what the values are so it is a statement open to wide interpretation and possible abuse. Interestingly, there is no parallel statement in the Standards for Teachers in Scotland illustrating how divergent policy can quickly become.

Do other countries have a legal requirement to promote their country's values, and if yes, what might be included in such a policy?

The influence that political agendas should have on education policy is a 'wicked problem'. Rittel and Webber (1973, p. 155) consider a wicked problem to be one which is, 'difficult to define; has no single solution; unique and may be the symptom of other problems'. Within the sociocultural context of education, the wickedness arises from the multiple influences at play in society and the formulation of an education system that will satisfy all the stakeholders. Whose voice should be heard above all the rest? A government is elected to run the country in the best interests of its citizens. The issue is how is it possible for the government to listen and respond to every point of view on the issue of educational policy?

The *Sydney Morning Herald* of 17 April 2017 published an article about the abolition of the Safe Schools programme in NSW (2017), which informed students about the effects of bullying and how to combat it. It was abolished because the state government considered the programme to be social engineering. The author, Haydar, commented that the same government insists on retaining the teaching of scripture in schools, against the advice given in a report that they commissioned. The article highlights the contradiction in these decisions because both school programmes could be viewed as forms of social engineering. One is not acceptable to the government but the other is.

What other 'wicked problems' do teachers experience?

Maybe there is no solution to the policy imposition dilemma. There are many 'wicked problems' which confront all of us involved in education, and often it is those who are responsible for the daily provision of education to the nation's children and young people who have to make such difficult decisions.

Further reading

Allen, J. (ed.) (2004) *Sociology of Education: Possibilities and Practices*, Melbourne: Cengage, *Section Seven: Social Change and Education*.

Australian Curriculum Assessment and Reporting Authority (ACARAa) (n.d.) *Australian Curriculum*. Available at: https://www.acara.edu.au/curriculum (Accessed April 2018).

Australian Curriculum Assessment and Reporting Authority (ACARAb) (n.d.) NAPLAN Available at: https://www.nap.edu.au/naplan (Accessed April 2018).

Churchill, R., Ferguson, P., Godinho, S., Johnson, N., Keddie, A., Letts, W., and Vick, M. (2011) *Teaching: Making a Difference, Part 1: The Teaching Profession*, Milton: John Wiley.

Delors, J. (1996) *Learning: The Treasure Within*, Paris: United Nations Educational Scientific and Cultural Organization.

Department for Education (2011) *Prevention and Reduction: A Review of Strategies for Intervening Early to Prevent or Reduce Youth Crime and Anti-Social Behaviour*. Available from http://dera.ioe.ac.uk/3588/1/3588_DFE-RR111.pdf (Accessed November 2018).

Galey, S. (2015) 'Education Politics and Policy: Emerging Institutions, Interests, and Ideas', *Policy Studies Journal*, 43, S12–S39. doi:10.1111/psj.12100.

Groundwater-Smith, S., Ewing, R., and Cornu, R. (2011) 'Teaching, Learning and Curriculum in a Changing World', Chapter 6 in *Teaching Challenges and Dilemmas*, Melbourne: Cengage.

Haydar, N. (2017) *Safe Schools Programme Ditched in NSW* (Australian Broadcast Corporation) at http://www.abc.net.au/news/2017-04-16/safe-schools-program-ditched-in-nsw/8446680 (Accessed April 2018).

Kalantzis, M., and Cope, B. (2009) *New Learning: Elements of a Science of Education, Part A: Introduction – Changing Education*, Melbourne: Cambridge University Press.

Ministerial Council on Education Employment Training and Youth Affairs (MCEETY) (2008) *Melbourne Declaration on Educational Goals for Young Australians*, Melbourne: Curriculum Corporation.

Rennie, L., Venville, G., and Wallace, J. (2012) *Knowledge That Counts in a Global Community*, Abingdon: Routledge.

Rittel, H., and Weber, M. (1973) 'Dilemmas in a General Theory of Planning', *Policy Sciences*, 4, pp. 155–69.

UK Government (2011) *Teachers' Standards*. (DFE-00066-2011) Available at: https://assets.publishing.service.gov.uk/government/uploads/system/uploads/attachment_data/file/665520/Teachers__Standards.pdf (Accessed April 2018).

5

What are the effects of changing curriculums?

The nuances of a new primary mathematics curriculum in Malaysia

Mas Norbany binti Abu Samah

In 2011, a new national education curriculum was introduced in Malaysia to meet the demands to improve the quality of primary mathematics education by making it more relevant to the twenty-first century. The aims were to develop human capital, to have creative open-minded pupils who develop into world-class thinkers and to nurture the spirit of the nation. As a result, the emphasis for the mathematics curriculum and assessments has been on mastery of knowledge and application of school-based assessment.

In 1994 the Primary School Integrated Curriculum was introduced. The Kurikulum Bersepadu Sekolah Rendah (KBSR) included mathematics. Its aim was to train pupils to master not only calculating skills but also a requirement to foster an honourable and responsible attitude in daily activities. It was introduced to improve and develop pupils understanding of number concepts as well as acquiring basic calculation skills. In addition, pupils would learn to appreciate mathematics. The mathematical knowledge gained would also help pupils to manage their daily activities systematically, thus fulfilling the requirement of our society and nation to progress, as well as help our pupils to further their knowledge.

In 2011, the Kurikulum Standard Sekohah Rendah (KSSR) was introduced, initially into Year One. Changes in the content included 'Content Standards', 'Learning Standards'. 'Performance Standards' and the types of assessment used which had an 'authentic and holistic' approach. The aim of this curriculum is to prepare pupils with the skills and pedagogy relevant to the latest development for social and economic needs. It is also to prepare the students with relevant knowledge, skills and values as human capital; to be students who are highly creative, innovative and critical, aligned with the challenges of the twenty-first century. KSSR is an improved version of KBSR, which stresses the importance of reaching the standards of the content as well as the standards of learning to be attained in terms of measurable performance against assessment criteria.

The current mathematics curriculum is related to the study of how children learn and apply mathematics as well as examining how learning is influenced and developed through teaching strategies (Nik Azis, 2008). Since the nineteenth century the mathematics curriculum has evolved considerably. The linking and cross-referencing of learning theory, teaching methods, assessment and research has been formulated to help mathematics teachers relate theory to practice and enable them to practise reflective skills (Seow, 1995). In the early twentieth century, curriculum development emerged as an important issue within an educational crisis (Abdul Rahim Hamdan, 2007). Nations such as Japan, Singapore, Korea and Malaysia decided to evaluate the education curriculum including the transformation and reformation of the mathematics curriculum (Usiskin et al., 2008). This curriculum change was influenced by various key factors: Western philosophy, Islamic philosophy, the need to increase human capital in the private sector, industrial research and development and the need to train and educate the workforce (Glenn, 2000; Glenn and Gordon, 2004; Hass, 1987).

How do the aims of your country's mathematics curriculum compare with those of Malaysia?

Mathematics education has undergone several reformations and transformations following the rapid changes in the social and cultural system of the multicultural population of Malaysia. The Prime Minister Dato' Seri Najib Tun Abdul Razak (2013) stated that education transformation needs to be implemented to produce a generation that can think out of the box.

Curriculum change needs to be implemented to produce pupils who can function effectively, have high moral values, are creative and productive in the process of maintaining a harmonious and united nation and meets national development that is in line with the Razak Report (1956), Rahman Taib Report (1960), 1961 Education Act and the Cabinet Committee Report (1979).

How might you promote creative, critical and innovative thinkers in your mathematics classroom?

The style of teaching has changed. There is a move away from rote learning and achievement through competition. There is a greater emphasis on interactive activities and a more informal approach. Learning through games, songs and practical resources is encouraged. The intention is to make learning more meaningful and fun and thus more effective. A particular inclusion in the new curriculum is the expectation of children to use reasoning and offer opinion in lessons and to learn to be accountable for their actions. For example, a lesson on money will be combined with input on the value and use of money.

The content of the KSSR Mathematics Programme (Assessment and Standards Curriculum Document, 2011) is aimed at developing one of the basic mathematical skills, namely the counting skills among students. The pupils are guided to develop the counting skills through quantitative thinking based on logical steps. The development of counting skill is strengthened in solving quantitative, measuring, rounding up, estimation, reading of tables, easy graph formulation and data handling. The skill is also developed by communicating quantitatively using mathematical language which will enable students to understand a few patterns and characteristics of numbers using decimal numbers and motivate students to learn.

Traditionally, Malaysia has had an exam-orientated system of assessment. Streaming students is no longer an expectation and even collaborative assessments are acceptable. The assessment in KSSR Mathematics (Performance Standard in KSSR, 2011) can be divided into three forms, namely the formative, summative and progress assessments (Nik Azis Nik Pa, 1992). Currently, the School-Based Assessment (SBA) is the focus of education in Malaysia. Testing is used normally as the classroom assessment strategy. An alternative strategy to testing is needed as a reference for teachers in ensuring a balanced human capital that could face the current and future challenges can be produced.

The formative assessment is implemented to give feedback of the teaching and learning process (Black et al., 2003). This assessment aims to decide whether the pupils have mastered a particular skill which is totally in line with the learning objective in terms of the cognitive, affective and psychomotor aspects. A teacher has to identify the strengths and weaknesses in these aspects and takes follow-up actions to increase the effectiveness of the teaching and learning of mathematics. An assessment provides information about the student's achievement in knowledge and skill, interest and creativity developments, attitude change, internalization of values, practical ability and psychomotor skill. The formative format of assessment is conducted after the students have learnt a particular basic mathematics skill thus enabling the teacher to take direct follow-up actions to overcome any problem. The summative assessment is used to detect the students' achievement in general at the end of several units of mathematics education. The aim of this type of assessment is to enable the students' grade of achievement to be recorded in the Student Profile Record. Besides this, the teacher also implements the progress assessment to detect the students' progress level which is recorded in the students' Performance Record. Based on these results, the teacher will plan for enrichment and remedial activities for students (Nik Azis, 2002).

In your own country, how is primary mathematics assessed?

Through the problem-solving process, pupils will be able to build mathematical knowledge and concepts. Through the communication process, the students will be able to explain and strengthen mathematical understanding, to present mathematical ideas clearly and coherently to peers and teachers. The teacher acts as an analyst and evaluates mathematical thinking. The KSSR curriculum also involves the mathematical reasoning process as the basis for understanding mathematics effectively. Students are able to make conjectures, prove the conjectures, provide logical explanation, analyse, make considerations, evaluate and provide justifications for all mathematical activities. Besides that, the belief that mathematics is all about a set procedure or algorithm that needs to be learnt to solve problems is untrue. KSSR is also related to the process of relating the conceptual and procedural knowledge. The topics in mathematics are not only related to each other but also connected to other fields. KSSR is also related to the process of making representations where students are able to create and use the representations to organize, record and communicate mathematical ideas. Students also have to choose, apply and translate mathematical representations to solve problems and to communicate the mathematical method, understanding and debates to themselves and to others (KSSR Curriculum Specification, 2011).

What would you consider is needed to help teachers deliver an ambitious mathematics curriculum?

KSSR Mathematics also lays stress on numeracy, building and measuring, operating and analysing data, arithmetic manipulation, algebraic manipulation, using algorithm, using mathematical tools and ICT skills. These mathematical skills additionally refer to the ability to use the appropriate mathematical language and apply the mathematical ideas, test and prove conjectures, extract meaning from mathematical writing and using mathematics to explain the physical world. KSSR Mathematics also develops the analytical skill in terms of the ability to think clearly, give attention to and scrutinize every aspect, manipulate detailed and correct ideas, understand complex mathematical reasoning, construct and defend logical ideas and debate the inappropriate ones. KSSR Mathematics has provided the Content Standard (CS), which is the general statement about the affective and cognitive domains attainable by the students in each subtopic, arranged according to the concept building hierarchy. CS should be realistic and suitable according to the students' age and ability. Learning Standard (LS) refers to the specific statement with regard to what the students know and are able to do in terms of knowledge and ability to show their proficiency in obtaining measurable knowledge, skill and values (KSSR Curriculum Specification, 2011).

The Standard-Based Curriculum Primary School (KSSR) implemented in 2011 is in line with the steps taken by several countries that have reviewed their education systems. Countries such as Australia, the United Kingdom, Singapore and Korea. In general, curriculum change is aimed at providing a platform for national education that meets future challenges and this transformation is intended to produce students who can effectively function in the future. Changes and adaptations in this curriculum display a better curriculum development (Liberman et al., 2012; Cross City Campaign for Urban School Reform, 2005; Timperley and Parr, 2005; Cohen and Hill, 2001; Ball and Cohen, 1999).

How has your mathematics curriculum adapted to the requirements of the twenty-first century?

Implementation of the new curriculum demands that teachers be better prepared to realize the requirements of the curriculum. The constructs of availability, acceptance and monitoring practices are fundamental in ensuring that the new curriculum can be implemented effectively by the teacher. In conclusion, the mathematics curriculum worldwide has undergone tremendous change, reformed to ensure a greater mastery of mathematical concepts, to be in line with a changing world. The primary mission in Malaysia is to produce students who are capable of effectively mastering and applying mathematics in the everyday of this world.

Further reading

Ball, D., and Cohen, D. (1999) 'Developing Practice, Developing Practitioners: Toward a Practice-Based Theory of Professional Education', in Darling-Hammond, L. and Sykes, G. (eds), *Teaching as the Learning Profession*, San Francisco: Jossey-Bass, pp. 3–32.

Black, P., Harrison, C., Lee, C., Marshall, B., and William, D. (2003) *Assessment for Learning: Putting It into Practice*, Maidenhead: Open University Press.

Cabinet Committee (1979) *Mengkaji Dasar Pelajaran*, Kuala Lumpur: Dewan Bahasa dan Pustaka.

Chua Yan Piaw (2006) *Kaedah Penyelidikan*, Kuala Lumpur: Mc Graw Hill.

Cohen, D., and Hill, H. (2001) *Learning Policy*, New Haven: Yale University Press.

Cross City Campaign for Urban School Reform (2005) *A Delicate Balance: District Policies and Classroom Practice*, Chicago: Cross City Campaign for Urban School Reform.

Education Act (1961) Kuala Lumpur: MDC Sdn. Bhd.

Fraenkel, J., and Wallen, N. (1996) *How to Design and Evaluate Research in Education* (edisi ketiga), New York: McGraw Hill.

Gagne, R., and Briggs, L. (eds.) (1979) *Principles of Instructional Design*, New York: Holt, Rinehart and Winston.

Glenn, J. (2000) *Before It's Too Late: A Report to the Nation from the National Commission on Mathematics and Science Teaching for the 21st Century*. Washington, DC: Department of Education. Available at: https://eric.ed.gov/?id=ED441705 (Accessed November 2018).

Glenn, J., and Gordon, T. J. (2004) *State of the Future at the Millennium*, Washington DC: American Council for the United Nations University.

Habsah Ismail (2000) 'Kefahaman Guru Tentang Konsep Pendidikan Bersepadu Dalam Kurikulum Bersepadu Sekolah Menengah (KBSM)' PhD Thesis, Universiti Kebangsaan Malaysia.

Hamdan Rahim Abdul (2007) *Pengajian kurikulum*, Kuala Lumpur: Penerbit Universiti Teknologi Malaysia.

Hass, G. (1987) *Curriculum Planning: A New Approach*, Boston, MA: Allyn.

Hassan, N. (2004) *Hubungan Antara Pengguna Bahan Bantu Mengajar Dengan Minat Pelajar Tingkatan Lima Sekolah Menengah Kem, Pengkalan Chepa, Kelantan*, Universiti Pendidikan Sultan Idris.

Liberman, N., David K., and Beeri, C. (2012) 'Regressed Experts as a New State in Teacher Professional Development: Lessons from Computer Science Teacher, Adjustments to Substantial Changes in the Curriculum', *Journal of Computer Science Education*, 22:3, pp. 237–55.

Manta Musak (1993) 'Moral Values in Malaysian Integrated School Curriculum: A Survey on Teachers Perception and Abilities' (PhD Thesis), University of South Dakota.

Ministry of Education, Malaysia (2011) KSSR: *Assessment and Standard Curriculum Document*, Malaysia: Ministry of Education.

Ministry of Education, Malaysia (2011) KSSR: *Curriculum Specification*, Malaysia: Ministry of Education.

Ministry of Education (1994) *Kurikulum Bersepadu Sekolah Rendah* (KBSR) (Primary School Integrated Curriculum), Malaysia: Ministry of Education.

Ministry of Education (2011) *Kurikulum Standard Sekolah Rendah* (KSSR) (Primary School Integrated Curriculum), Malaysia: Ministry of Education.

Nik Azis Nik Pa (1992) *Penghayatan Matematik KBSR & KBSM*, Kuala Lumpur: Dewan Bahasa dan Pustaka.

Nik Azis Nik Pa (1997) *Pendidikan Moral dan Nilai di Malaysia: Satu analisis tentang konsep dan realiti dari perspektif bersepadu*, Prosiding Pendidikan Moral dan Nilai, hlm, pp. 127–46.

Nik Azis Nik Pa (2002) *Penghayatan Matematik, Perkembangan Professional, KBSR dan KBSM*, Kuala Lumpur: Dewan Bahasa dan Pustak.

Nik Azis Nik Pa (2008) *Isu-isu kritikal dalam pendidikan Matematik*, Kuala Lumpur: Penerbitan Universiti Malaya.

Ong, A.-C. (2004) *Teaching Strategies That Promote Thinking*, Singapura: McGraw-Hill.

Rahman Taib (1960) *First Malaysian Plan 1966–1970*, Kuala Lumpur: Percetakan Kerajaan.

Seow, S. (1995) *Pengajaran Matematik, KBSR*, Selangor: Fajar bakti Sdn Bhd.

Timperley, H., and Parr, J. (2005) 'Theory Competition and the Process of Change', *Journal of Educational Change*, 6:3, pp. 227–51.

Tun Abdul Razak (1956) *Report of the Education Committee 1956*. Kuala Lumpur: Government Press. Available at: http://www.fccmsm.org/wp-content/uploads/2015/01/Razak-Report-1956.pdf (Accessed November 2018).

Usiskin, Z., and Willmore, E. (eds) (2008) *Mathematics Curriculum in Pacific Rim Countries-China, Japan, Korea and Singapore*, Charlotte, NC: Information Age.

Wiersma, W. (2000) *Research Method in Education: An Introduction*, Boston: Allyn and Bacon.

Wright, D. (1995) 'Mnemonics: An Aid to Geographical Learning, Teacher's Notebook', *Journal of Education*, 94:1, pp. 339–40.

Yusup Hashim dan Razmah Man (ed.) (1993) *Teknologi Instruksi: Teori dan Aplikasi*. Tanjong Malim: Universiti Pendidikan Sultan Idris.

6

Are there strategies that provide successful inclusion for all students in general education?

Examining the implementation in the United States of a project designed to support children with disabilities

Ellen Warrington

In the United States, every child is provided with public schooling from Kindergarten through to Grade 12 (ages five to nineteen). Students who have been identified with a disability may also be covered under the Individuals with Disabilities Education Improvement Act (IDEIA). This entitles them to access to the general education curriculum while having their unique needs met. How this is managed depends upon the individual student and the Individual Education Plan (IEP) team. A necessary component of each IEP is the Least Restrictive Environment (LRE), which is assumed as the general education classroom, at least to start the discussion of placement and services. As more school districts and IEP teams insist that the LRE for students with disabilities is indeed the general education classroom, strategies and training are essential to aid general classroom instructors in this inclusive effort. An additional challenge is to meet the needs of students who are unable to learn from conventional methods and struggle in the classroom (Meyer and Rose, 2005). Instructors are tasked with finding ways for students to engage with and master the content they present.

In your experience, what effective structures are in place to support individual needs?

Universal Design for Learning (UDL) is one strategy that addresses the barriers faced by students who struggle to learn for whatever reason. Using UDL in the general education classroom requires little additional accommodation or modification, no matter what the range of learning needs might be. UDL is defined by the Centre for Universal Design in the United States as 'the design of products and environments to be usable by all people, to the greatest extent possible, without the need for adaptation or specialized design' (cited by Burgstahler, 2015). It is about designing resources, curricula and the classroom environment in ways that help students' master content less accessible under conventional methods (Meyer and Rose, 2005), whatever their needs. Content may be customized for individual students through the use of technology and instructors can incorporate a variety of ways through which students can engage and interact with the material. By reducing presentation barriers, UDL makes 'accessibility of content' the forefront of planning and a focus for instructors so they can be proactive in their planning to engage students at the highest level possible (McGuire et al., 2003).

Many see implementing UDL in the general education classroom as a daunting challenge; it requires meticulous planning and creation beforehand, which initially means more work. However, once the planning and creation are completed the benefits to instructor and students are worth the efforts (Dell et al., 2015). This preparation includes consideration of the multiple ways in which the students are engaging in and interacting with the curriculum. Rather than the creation of a single mode of delivery of information, a single assessment and a single manner for engaging with the material, the instructor must think about how s/he might undertake the teaching role using multiple modes of each principle.

Under the first principle, that of 'multiple means of representing material/information', instructors consider the possibilities of delivery of content, thinking about the ways in which students learn, such as visually or practically. Material can be adjusted to match the cognitive learning styles of the students in the classroom (Firchow, 2016). Incorporating these methods of delivery into one's teaching requires a shift in mindset, particularly if the instructor tended towards a lecturing style in the past. The instructor might consider the use of video or graphs to present material so that students are interacting with the information using multiple senses (Meyer and Rose, 2005). Music might be incorporated into the presentation of content. Instructors will support the various paths that students will take to engage with the curriculum materials. A specific example of implementing UDL in the representation principle would be to provide students in your maths class with the opportunity to view a video which contains problem solving for fractions. The students might also complete a simulation actually using fractions in a real-world situation, such as baking or in building. Using any of these strategies allows students who are mostly bimodal in learning style (visual and auditory) to engage with the material at a deeper level (Pisha and Coyne, 2001). Each student will be afforded the scaffolding needed to engage and interact in a way that results in successful completion and understanding of the concepts presented (Hitchcock et al., 2002).

In what ways could you practically adjust presentation of teaching materials to widen access to learning?

Students can have models of skilled performance at their disposal to use as a reference for their own practices. Students will receive feedback frequently about their performance as well as the manner in which they are engaging with the content and materials for the curriculum. If done well, the planning will include real-world applications that give students ample opportunity to practice the skills being learned in meaningful contexts (Hitchcock et al. 2002).

The second principle, 'multiple means of expression', allows students to demonstrate what they have learned using one of a variety of ways. Under the UDL approach, the assessment is suited to the task as well as the means (Meyer and Rose 2005). Rather than the instructor creating a single test or project for the end of a unit or chapter, for example, the students are offered a choice of two or three different paths of assessment to demonstrate their learning. A specific example for this principle of expression might be when a teacher allows his/her students to choose from one of the following options when presenting information researched to the class: oral presentation, video presentation or written presentation. This allows for flexibility, individualized student learning style and expression and increased potential for successful completion of the content. Moreover, and of great importance, the multiple means of expression used for assessment purposes can provide more accurate knowledge of the progress students are making than a single mode may afford (Hitchcock et al., 2002). As instructors, it is important to know whether the assessment task assesses a student's ability to engage with that form of assessment (such as a media type for a film product,) alongside the content being assessed.

What are the advantages and disadvantages of providing different assessment modes for individuals of the same content?

The third principle, 'multiple means of engagement', recognizes in its intent that students often have their own motivation for learning as well as an ability to engage with the learning and materials. Again, offering student choice by allowing more than one option for ways to access material affords possibilities for further student involvement and thus, success. An example might be providing students with a video of the instructor's lecture to view outside the class so the student is able to review as often as needed to grasp the key concepts (Meyer and Rose, 2005). Another specific example might be providing students with real-world examples of job requirements to engage students in career skills. Additional resources can be offered to students, facilitating the various levels of repetition and practice required by individuals. Students who prefer reading about a subject can choose that pathway to access the content. Others might prefer to look at visual images, such as pictures or video, to enhance their understanding of the content. Still others may prefer to listen to someone, perhaps the instructor, lecture about the content to add to their understanding. Having all of these options available to students to choose from as they engage with new concepts can be motivating and increase opportunities to succeed (Hitchcock et al., 2002). When educators speak about access to the curriculum, the emphasis is on how we plan for learning and make it relevant and comprehensible to all students (Hitchcock et al., 2002).

How might this approach be accommodated in one topic? Consider a variety of mediums.

Using the principles of UDL as the foundation for the curriculum, instructors allow for those students with visual, auditory, reading or other kinds of learning issues to interact with the materials in their preferred ways, as often as they need. The flexibility enables students to demonstrate their knowledge of the content through their chosen mode of assessment (Hitchcock et al., 2002). Although there appear to be many benefits and positives of UDL, there are some concerns with this approach too. Many educators believe that in order to implement UDL there has to be access to large amounts of technology. Some technology may indeed enhance students' interaction with materials outside of class, but the level of technology required varies with teacher creativity (Meyer and Rose, 2005). Indeed, there are options available that require very little technology.

How should technology be integrated into teaching and particularly to meet individual needs?

Further concerns include the amount of time required for advanced preparation prior to implementation. Starting small has been the answer for many who have initiated UDL in their classrooms (Noonoo, 2014). Instructors who have chosen to start small selected either one assessment with which to work, a chapter or module in which to implement UDL as a project or a different delivery mode. An important aspect to implementation is the reflection that occurs before planning what will be delivered. It is critical that the instructor considers the students in her or his class, identifying their individual needs for learning. This is the guiding foundation upon which to build UDL teaching, an essential first step if the work and effort teachers' invest is to have positive outcomes on student learning.

Further reading

The Centre for Universal Design (CUD), cited by Burgstahler, S. (2015) Universal Design: Process, Principles, and Applications. Available at: https://www.washington.edu/doit/sites/default/files/atoms/files/Universal_Design%20Process%20Principles%20and%20Applications.pdf (Accessed July 2018).

Dell, C., Dell, T., and Blackwell, T. (2015) 'Applying Design for Learning in Online Courses: Pedagogical and Practical Considerations', *Journal of Educators Online*, 13:2, pp. 166–92. Available at: http://files.eric.ed.gov/fulltext/EJ1068401.pdf/ (Accessed January 2018).

Firchow, N. (2016) 'Universal Design for Learning–Improved Access for All', Available at: http://www.greatschools.org/gk/articles/universal-design-for-learning-improved-access-for-all/ (Accessed December 2016).

Hitchcock, C., Meyer, A., Rose, D., and Jackson, R. (2002) 'Providing New Access to the General Curriculum: Universal Design for Learning', *Council for Exceptional Children*, 35:2, pp. 8–17.

Individuals with Disabilities Education Improvement Act. Available at: https://sites.ed.gov/idea/statuteregulations/ (Accessed January 2018).

McGuire, J., Scott, S., and Shaw, S. (2003) 'Universal Design for Instruction: The Paradigm, Its Principles, and Products', *Journal on Postsecondary Education and Disability*, 17:1, pp. 11–21.

Meyer, A., and Rose. D. (2005) 'The Future is in the Margins: The Role of Technology and Disability in Educational Reform'. Available at: http://www.udlcenter.org/sites/udlcenter.org/files/Meyer-Rose_FutureisintheMargins_2.pdf/ (Accessed January 2018).

Noonoo, S. (2014) '6 Ways to Engage Every Learner Using UDL', *THE Journal*. Available at: https://thejournal.com/articles/2014/12/03/6-ways-to-engage-every-learner-using-udl.aspx/ (Accessed January 2018).

Pisha, B., and Coyne, P. (2001) 'Smart from the Start. The Promise of Universal Design for Learning', *Remedial and Special Education*, 22:4, pp. 197–203.

7

Can diversity really be used in teaching minority language students?

A social and cultural approach to the integration of indigenous children in Canada

Lynne Wiltse

Although Canadian classrooms are increasingly linguistically and culturally diverse spaces, with Indigenous populations in particular on the rise, pre-service and in-service teachers remain predominantly white, monolingual and middle class (Mujawamariya and Mahrouse, 2004; Ryan et al., 2009). This reality necessitates a call for pedagogies that consider diversity as a resource (Schecter and Cummins, 2003) rather than as a deficit. Despite promising approaches, such as a 'funds of knowledge' (Moll et al., 1992) perspective that encourages educators to make connections between children's out-of-school lives and school learning, researchers argue that many schools and teachers know so little about the out-of-school lives of their students, particularly for minority language learners, that they find it difficult to build on funds of knowledge from children' s homes and communities (Gunderson, 2006;

Marshall and Toohey, 2010, Smythe and Toohey, 2009). This is of concern, as underachievement remains high among minority learners, in particular for students from indigenous backgrounds and immigrant students whose first language is different from the dominant language of school and society (Cummins et al., 2015). These students are typically characterized by what they lack and given remedial instruction that does not require the use of higher level thinking skills. Rather, in this chapter I recommend teaching practices that consider students' multilingual skills and cultural backgrounds as academic resources.

Why do you think deficit perspectives of minority language students are so common?

The case profiled in this chapter highlights select findings from a three-year-school-university collaborative research study in Western Canada that investigated ways to improve indigenous and other minority language students' access to school literacy practices. Within a broad sociocultural framework, the research was grounded in a funds of knowledge perspective and drew on the work of educational researchers who have used ethnographic studies to understand children's language and literacy practices, both in school (Comber, 2016; Wallace, 2005) and out-of-school (Schultz and Hull, 2002). This qualitative study involved three interconnected groups of research participants: (a) a teacher researcher study group comprised of three Indigenous teachers and three non-Indigenous teachers; (b) Indigenous students from the participating teachers' classes who were in Grades 4–7 (nine- to twelve-year-olds); (c) pre-service teachers from my language and literacy classes who were partnered with the students in literacy partnerships. It is important to note that three of the teachers taught ten- to eleven-year-olds at Wolfwood School (all names are pseudonyms), operated by the local First Nations band, whereas the other three taught the same grade at inner city public schools with significant numbers of Indigenous students. Teachers attended monthly meetings to explore pertinent sociocultural literature and discuss related classroom practice. The type of schools in which the teachers taught determined, to a considerable degree, how successful they were in integrating children's home languages, literacies and cultures into the school curriculum.

What effect may contrasting teaching settings have on minority language students?

Study findings showed that, because Wolfwood School was a community school that included programming in the local Indigenous language, history and culture, for many of the student participants there was little distance between out-of-school lives and in-school learning. This made it easier for teachers to draw on students' funds of knowledge in their teaching. However, this was seldom the case for the Indigenous students of the other teachers in the project. For example, during one of our monthly meetings, Les, who taught at one of the district schools, identified the 'disconnect between home for students and parents and the school community as a key issue' and 'finding ways to bridge that gap as absolutely critical'. During the same meeting, Eleanor, who taught at another district school, made a heartfelt acknowledgement to the Wolfwood School teachers: 'I think I should send all my First Nations children to your school, as they're getting short-changed with me. You use who the students are in your teaching and I think students would learn so much better that way.'

Rather than having students in Les's and Eleanor's classes move to Wolfwood School, what changes could teachers make to narrow the gap between children's out-of-school and in-school lives?

Terry, one of the teachers at Wolfwood School responded, 'I think something that our school does very well is give our students pride in who they are. When they go to high school, if they experience racism or have difficulties, they have some strength in being proud of who they are they are as a First Nations person.' Unfortunately, negative stereotypes about Indigenous peoples persist in the wider society, and Canadian research reports that Indigenous students continue to experience racism in school (Dion, 2007; Schick and St. Denis, 2005). As Wolfwood School only goes to Grade 7, students have to leave their community to attend high school. Given that, the significance of Terry's comment about affirming Indigenous students' identity cannot be overstated.

What are some strategies that teachers could use to support Indigenous, and other minority students, when they experience racism? How can racist attitudes be dealt with in productive ways?

To provide an example as to how students can reject negative stereotypes and at the same time 'construct identities of competence that fuel academic engagement' (Cummins et al., 2015, p. 559), I will briefly describe an initiative within the broader research study in which students at Wolfwood School participated. Participants created projects for Heritage Fair, a multimedia educational programme developed to increase awareness and interest in Canadian history and community and/or family culture. Some students took the opportunity to research prominent Indigenous Canadians, for instance, Phil Fontaine, the National Chief of the Assembly of First Nations at the time, and Dorothy Grant, an internationally renowned Indigenous fashion designer. Such topics provided students with opportunities to feel proud of their Indigenous heritage. The projects also allowed students to capitalize on their interests, in accordance with what Hedges, Cullen and Jordan (2011) refer to as 'funds of knowledge-based interests' (p. 198). For example, Darius completed his project on hunting, a traditional practice in his family and community. He explained his choice: 'I picked my project on hunting because it's part of my tradition. My grandfather and my uncle taught me. It's one of the things I most love to do … We hunt so we can feed our family with the meat.' Karina, a jingle dress dancer, explored the history and the practice of jingle dress dancing, a women's powwow dance, which originated from a dream among the Ojibwe people around 1900. Karina described the reasons for her choice: 'I picked this topic because I myself am a Jingle Dress dancer. I've been dancing at powwows since I was five, so I wanted to find more information on the Jingle Dress with this project.' These are just a few of the many projects that enabled students to examine and document linguistic and cultural practices in their local communities. To maximize the effectiveness of a funds of knowledge approach, it is best if teachers know the communities in which they work. For example, Gayle, the teacher of these students, was from the First Nations community, knew the students' families and had first-hand knowledge of many of the topics students' pursued. However, as Comber notes, '[s]ome teachers find themselves teaching in neighbourhoods where they themselves are strangers' (Comber, 2013, p. 361).

How can teachers be proactive so that they do not remain strangers in the communities in which they teach?

Teachers don't have to remain strangers. They need to make the effort to get to know their students and the communities in which they live so that they can use diversity as a resource, rather than consider it a deficit. On this note, study findings confirmed that involvement in the project increased teachers' awareness of the importance of utilizing minority students' funds of knowledge and provided them with ideas as to how to proceed in productive ways. For example, small steps were being made at Les's school: 'As part of a drumming unit, the music teacher encouraged First Nations students who had traditional drums to bring them to school. They did a presentation to the rest of the school that was well received. Plans are being made at the district level for the school to have a designated First Nations cultural space for students.' And, Eleanor had made progress: 'For me, this project has really been about how to acknowledge that my students, who are often from a very low socio-economic class, the First Nations kids and the Southeast Asian kids, are all bringing something a little different to school.' Rather than regarding this difference as a deficit, Eleanor gradually became aware of the educational value in 'using students' knowledge and prior experiences as a scaffold for new learning' (Amanti, 2005, p. 135). This realization holds promise for the many teachers who teach students from communities with which they are not familiar. As educators, we must do a better job of using diversity to teach language minority students; this chapter provides a glimpse as to how that can be achieved.

How will you use diversity as a resource in your teaching?

Further reading

Amanti, C. (2005) 'Beyond a Beads and Feathers Approach', in Gonzáles, N. Moll, L., and Amanti, C. (eds), *Funds of Knowledge: Theorizing Practices in Households, Communities and Classrooms*, London: Lawrence Erlbaum Associates, pp. 131–41.

Comber, B. (2013) 'Schools as Meeting Places: Critical and Inclusive Literacies in Changing Local Environments', *Language Arts*, 90:5, pp. 361–71.

Comber, B. (2016) *Literacy, Place and Pedagogies of Possibility*, London: Routledge.

Cummins, J., Chow, P., and Schecter, S. (2006) 'Community as Curriculum', *Language Arts*, 83:4, pp. 297–307.

Cummins, J., and Early, M. (eds) (2011) *Identity Texts: The Collaborative Creation of Power in Multilingual Schools*, Stoke-on-Trent: Trentham Books.

Cummins, J., and Early, M. (2015) *Big Ideas for Expanding Minds: Teaching English Language Learners Across the Curriculum*, Toronto: Rubicon Press/Pearson.

Cummins, J., Hu, S., Markus, P., and Montero, M. (2015) 'Identity Texts and Academic Achievement: Connecting the Dots in Multilingual School Contexts', *TESOL Quarterly*, 49:3, pp. 55–581.

Dagenais, D., Toohey, K., Bennett, A., and Singh, A. (2017) 'Multilingual and Multimodal Composition at School: Scribjab in Action', *Language and Education*, 31:3, pp. 263–82.

Dion, S. (2007) 'Disrupting Molded Images: Identities, Responsibilities and Relationships-Teachers and Indigenous Subject Material', *Teaching Education*, 18:4, pp. 329–42.

Gunderson, L. (2006) *English-Only Instruction and Immigrant Students in Secondary Schools: A Critical Examination*, Mahwah: Lawrence Erlbaum.

Hedges, H., Cullen, J., and Jordan, B. (2011) 'Early Years Curriculum: Funds of Knowledge as a Conceptual Framework for Children's Interests', *Journal of Curriculum Studies*, 43:2, pp. 185–205.

Marshall, E., and Toohey, K. (2010) 'Representing Family: Community Funds of Knowledge, Bilingualism, and Multimodality', *Harvard Education Review*, 80:2, pp. 221–41.

Moll, L., Amanti, C., Neff, D., and Gonzales, N. (1992) 'Funds of Knowledge for Teaching: Using a Qualitative Approach to Connect Homes and Classrooms', *Theory into Practice*, 31:2, pp. 132–41.

Mujawamariya, D., and Mahrouse, G. (2004) 'Multicultural Education in Canadian Preservice Programs: Teacher Candidates' Perspectives', *Alberta Journal of Educational Research*, 50:4, pp. 336–53.

Ryan, J., Pollock, K., and Antonelli, F. (2009) 'Teacher Diversity in Canada: Leaky Pipelines, Bottlenecks, and Glass Ceilings', *Canadian Journal of Education*, 32:3, pp. 591–617.

Schecter, S., and Cummins, J. (2003) *Multilingual Education in Practice: Using Diversity as a Resource*, Portsmouth: Heinemann.

Schick, C. and St. Denis, V. (2005) 'Troubling National Discourses in Anti-Racist Curricular Planning', *Canadian Journal of Education*, 28:3, pp. 295–317.

Schultz, K., and Hull, G. (eds) (2002) *School's Out! Bridging Out-of-School Literacies with Classroom Practice*, New York: Teachers College Press.

Smythe, S., and Toohey, K. (2009) 'Bringing Home and Community to School: What Can Schools do with Them?', in Kostogriz, A., Miller, J., and Gearon, M. (eds), *Linguistically and Culturally Diverse Classrooms: New Dilemmas for Teachers*, Bristol: Multilingual Matters, pp. 271–90.

Walker, D. (2014) *A Pedagogy of Powerful Communication: Youth Radio and Radio Arts in the Multilingual Classroom*, New York: Peter Lang.

Wallace, C. (2005) 'Conversations around the Literacy Hour in a Multilingual London Primary School', *Language and Education*, 19:4, pp. 146–61.

8

How can inclusion be promoted through a linguistically responsive pedagogy?

The recognition of the disconnect between 'home language' and school or 'academic language' and how this might be resolved in Finland

Jenni Alisaari, Heli Vigren and Leena Maria Heikkola

Why have a linguistically responsive pedagogy? Finnish education has an excellent global reputation due mostly to PISA results that report high achievement among Finnish adolescents. However, in the Finnish media, concerns about young people's literacy skills are increasing (see, e.g., Kaseva,

2017; Manninen, 2017; Torvinen, 2018). The reading habits of Finns have changed because of the frequent use of mobile devices for reading and writing in new contexts where texts are short (KTM, 2017). In addition, demographics in Finnish classrooms have started to change with a notable increase in linguistic diversity (Hämäläinen, 2018). Recent studies show that the learning outcomes of students with migrant backgrounds in Finland are considerably lower than those of native Finnish students (Harju-Luukkainen et al., 2014; Kuukka and Metsämuuronen, 2016; OECD, 2015; Vettenranta et al., 2016), and the Finnish language skills of students with migrant backgrounds are not sufficient for studying academic subjects (Kuukka and Metsämuuronen, 2016).

Effective literacy and academic language skills are key to ensuring educational equity for all learners (Beacco et al., 2015). If these skills are not achieved during basic education, students' possibilities to successfully complete upper secondary education are threatened. If students are unfamiliar with discipline-specific language, it can hinder their learning. Hence, every teacher has to take into account the challenges that language in different subjects poses, and the linguistic skills that students need to learn while studying different subjects. Lucas and Villegas (2011; 2013) suggest that teachers are responsible for guiding students into the language used in their specific subjects. This requires a new linguistically responsive pedagogy that benefits every student at school, but especially learners who are vulnerable due to non-sufficient language skills for studying subjects, particularly if teachers do not pay attention to the language demands of that subject (Beacco et al., 2015).

How can a core curriculum support linguistically responsive pedagogy and language awareness in schools?

The renewed Finnish Core Curriculum came into effect in 2016. One of the innovations in it was the emphasis placed on language awareness based on the visions of the European Center of Modern Languages (ECML) and the European Council (EC). To promote equity of schooling, both institutions promote linguistically responsive teaching as key to the academic success of students of all backgrounds.

The Finnish national Core Curriculum for basic education (National Agency for Education, 2014) embraces the notion that every teacher is a language teacher. In Finnish basic education, every teacher is expected to pay attention to the role of language use in their specific subject area and to use linguistically responsive pedagogy in order to support the learning of academic language of all students. Furthermore, the Finnish Core Curriculum says that in a linguistically responsive school, '[t]he instruction progresses from everyday language to the language of conceptual thinking' (National Agency for Education, 2014). In practice, the importance of language and language skills must be understood in all activities, from reading science textbooks to physical education activities. The curriculum also demands that language awareness is included in every school's operating culture. Moreover, the curriculum requires that linguistically responsive teachers understand the role that language plays in every student's growth, learning, collaboration, identity building and socialization into the society (National Agency for Education, 2014).

To make linguistically responsive teaching beneficial for every student, it has to be acknowledged and promoted at curriculum level. The new Finnish Core Curriculum provides teachers with macro-level support to advocate for their students' linguistic achievements.

How is a linguistically responsive pedagogy currently reflected in your setting?

How can a teacher be linguistically responsive? Linguistically responsive teachers understand that language plays an important role both in acquiring and applying knowledge, as well as in communication (Beacco et al., 2015; Lucas and Villegas 2011; 2013; Schleppegrell, 2016). Language cannot be separated from learning content. Focusing on language in different subject lessons will develop the learners' content competence at the same time as their language skills (Beacco et al., 2015). In order to achieve this, teachers have to consider what kind of language the learners are required to learn when studying and producing texts in different subjects: Do the learners need to be able to take notes when the teacher is speaking? Do they need to discuss the content of the subject with another student? Do they need to answer questions based on what they have read? A linguistically responsive teacher should also focus on the key vocabulary and linguistic structures of the subject they teach and pay attention to the linguistic issues that are likely to be challenging for their learners (Lucas et al., 2008).

What are some specific ways you think you could promote your students' language development in content classes?

A linguistically responsive teacher examines the challenges language poses and how language is used in different subjects which all have different textual genres. Additionally, teachers have to be aware of the kind of language skills the students need in order to be able to understand and follow an assignment given to them in class. Only when teachers are aware and have knowledge about the different functions of language, are they able to teach language and its functions to their students.

A linguistically responsive teacher understands how language develops and what issues must be taken into account when students learn the content of a subject via language that might not yet be at an advanced level (Lucas et al., 2008). It is typical that language development gradually progresses from basic everyday language to a more abstract language. Basic everyday language skills include the ability to talk about everyday things and topics that are familiar to the speakers, using familiar words and structures (Gibbons, 2002).

In order to cope with the school's textual world, every learner needs to become familiar with academic register, the particular ways that language is used in school (Beacco et al., 2015). It is essential for teachers to understand, how everyday basic language skills differ from academic language skills, and that it takes several years for academic language skills to develop fully (Cummins, 2000). Even though this is mainly relevant when teaching multilingual learners, it is important to note that nobody speaks in academic register from their birth – everybody has to learn the language of schooling when they start school. In order to succeed in school, learners need to be able to produce and interpret the spoken and written texts of different subjects, and they need guidance on how to do this through linguistically responsive pedagogy (Beacco et al., 2015).

Consider some of the specific linguistic barriers to be overcome in one subject you have taught? Additionally, how might you draw on students' native languages to support their learning?

What does the future look like? Despite the potential of the Core Curriculum, Aalto and Tarnanen (2015) claim that linguistically responsive teaching is not yet a very common part of Finnish teacher training. In addition, our recent research indicates that Finnish teachers lack the knowledge and skills related to linguistically responsive pedagogy, suggesting that they need professional development in linguistically responsive teaching (Alisaari et al,. in review). However, these results are from data gathered slightly before the current curriculum was implemented in the fall of 2016, and there is no new research yet on the influence of the curriculum requirements on teachers' pedagogical skills. There is a great possibility that future research will show more positive results as the Finnish Ministry of Education and

Culture, and Finnish National Agency of Education are funding several projects focusing on developing teachers' skills in linguistically responsive teaching both in pre-service teacher education as well as in professional development of in-service teachers.

Taking a wider perspective, the European Commission is currently renewing its recommendations for key competences for European citizens, and linguistically responsive pedagogy is at the centre of attention in this process. Additionally, another important topic under discussion is the future professional development of teachers. Thus, it looks as if, in the European context, linguistically responsive pedagogy is gaining popularity. However, it is important to gain additional knowledge on how teachers implement linguistically responsive pedagogy in their classrooms, and most importantly, how it influences the learning outcomes of their students, measured for example by the PISA studies. Looking at the PISA results, we will possibly be able to follow the effects of linguistically responsive teaching in European countries and globally, in the OECD countries.

In your experience, to what extent is linguistic skill currently reflected in test results?

The knowledge gained over the past couple of decades regarding the benefits of linguistically responsive teaching shows that it has the potential to benefit every student in every classroom. In this way, linguistically responsive pedagogy can promote more inclusive education and increase all students' possibilities for success in wider society. This critical issue has at its core an equitable future for all our students: our job as teachers is to provide students with knowledge without allowing language to be a barrier.

Further reading

Aalto, E., and Tarnanen, M. (2015) 'Kielitietoinen aineenopetus opettajankoulutuksessa', in Kalliokoski, J., Mård-Miettinen, K., and Nikula, T. (eds), *Kieli koulutuksen resurssina: vieraalla ja toisella kielellä oppimisen ja opetuksen näkökulmia*. AFinLA-e. Soveltavan kielitieteen tutkimuksia 8, pp. 72–90. Available at: https://journal.fi/afinla/article/view/53773 (Accessed March 2018).
Alisaari, J., Heikkola, L., and Acquah, E. (in review) 'Kielitietoisuutta vai empatiaa? Opettajien käsityksiä kielestä ja kielitaidon kehittymisestä'. Submitted in *Kasvatus*.

Beacco, J.-C., Fleming, M., Goullier, F., Thürmann, E., and Vollmer, H. (2015) *The Language Dimension in All Subjects. A Handbook for Curriculum Development and Teacher Training*, Language Policy Unit. DGII – Directorate General of Democracy. Council of Europe. Available at: http://www.ecml.at/Portals/1/documents/CoE-documents/Handbook-Scol_final_EN.pdf (Accessed March 2018).

Cummins, J. (2000) *Language, Power and Pedagogy: Bilingual Children in the Crossfire*, Clevedon: Multilingual Matters.

Harju-Luukkainen, H., Nissinen, K., Sulkunen, S., Suni, M., and Vettenranta J. (2014) *Avaimet osaamisen tulevaisuuteen. Selvitys maahanmuuttajataustaisten nuorten osaamisesta ja siihen liittyvistä taustatekijöistä PISA 2012 -tutkimuksessa*, University of Jyväskylä, Finnish Institute for Educational Research. Available at: https://jyx.jyu.fi/dspace/handle/123456789/44290. (Accessed March 2018).

Hämäläinen, V. (2018) '*Vieraskieliset_kunnittain_2013_2017*', Personal information from Statistics of Finland, 12 January.

Kaseva, T. (2017) 'Pisa-menestyksen takana vaanii nurja puoli: tuhannet suomalaisnuoret lukevat niin surkeasti, etteivät selviä arjen tilanteista – miten se on mahdollista?' *Helsingin Sanomat*, Sunnuntai, 1 October [Online]. Available at: https://hs.fi/sunnuntai/art-2000005388591.html (Accessed February 2018).

KTM (2017) *Kansallinen mediatutkimus*. Available at: http://www.aikakauslehdet.fi/kmt/ (Accessed February 2018).

Kuukka, K., and Metsämuuronen, J. (2016) *Perusopetuksen päättövaiheen suomi toisena kielenä (S2) -oppimäärän oppimistulosten arviointi 2015*, Kansallinen koulutuksen arviointikeskus. Julkaisut 13:2016. Available at: https://karvi.fi/publication/perusopetuksen-paattovaiheen-suomi-toisena-kielena-s2-oppimaaran-oppimistulosten-arviointi-2015/ (Accessed March 2018).

Lucas, T., Villegas, A., and Freedson-Gonzalez, M. (2008) 'Linguistically Responsive Teacher Education: Preparing Classroom Teachers to Teach English Language Learners', *Journal of Teacher Education*, 59:4, pp. 361–73.

Lucas, T., and Villegas, A. (2011) 'A Framework for Preparing Linguistically Responsive Teachers', in Lucas, T. (ed.), *Teacher Preparation for Linguistically Diverse Classrooms: A Resource for Teacher Educators*, New York: Routledge, pp. 55–72.

Lucas, T., and Villegas, A. (2013) 'Preparing Linguistically Responsive Teachers: Laying the Foundation in Preservice Teacher Education', *Theory into Practice* 52, pp. 98–109.

Manninen, L. (2017) 'Asiantuntijoiden pysäyttävä huolenaihe koululaisista: tuhansilla oppilailla heikko lukutaito "Se uhkaa syrjäyttää ihmisen"',

Ilta-Sanomat, Kotimaa, 5 October [Online]. Available at: https://www.is.fi/kotimaa/art-2000005395586.html (Accessed March 2018).

National Agency for Education (2014) *Perusopetuksen opetussuunnitelman perusteet.* Määräykset ja ohjeet 2014:96, Available at: http://www.oph.fi/saadokset_ja_ohjeet/opetussuunnitelmien_ja_tutkintojen_perusteet/perusopetus (Accessed March 2018).

OECD (2015) *PISA in Focus: Can the Performance Gap between Immigrant and Non-immigrant Students Be Closed?* Available at: www.oecd-ilibrary.org/education/can-theperformance-gap-between-immigrant-and-nonimmigrant-students-be-closed_5jrxqs8mv327-en (Accessed March 2018).

Schleppegrell, M. (2006) 'The Challenges of Academic Language in School Subjects', in I. Lindberg and K. Sandwall (eds), *Språket och kunskapen: att lära på sitt andraspråk i skola och högskola*, pp. 47–69, Göteborg: Göteborgs universitet institutet för svenska som andraspråk.

Torvinen, P. (2018) 'Yksi kuva näyttää suomalaisten nuorten miesten osaamisen laskun, ja se on pysäyttävä – syitä ei tunneta', *Helsingin Sanomat*, 24 January. Available at: https://www.hs.fi/nyt/art-2000005537367.html?share=46b111e9c6ebdb2372a2491272481c31 (Accessed February 2018).

Vettenranta, J., Välijärvi, J., Ahonen, A., Hautamäki, J., Hiltunen, J., Leino, K., Lähteinen, S., Nissinen, K., Nissinen, V., Puhakka, E., Rautopuro, J., and Vainikainen, M.-P. (2016) *Huipulla pudotuksesta huolimatta. PISA 2015 -ensituloksia.* Opetus- ja kulttuuriministeriön julkaisuja 2016:41. Available at: https://ktl.jyu.fi/pisa/ajankohtaista/PISAjulkistaminen-2015 (Accessed March 2018).

9

How much does teacher enthusiasm affect student learning?

A finely observed research study on the relationship between student and teacher in relation to motivation in a Maltese college

Maria Mifsud

My interest in English Language Teaching (ELT) motivation was triggered by my constant search for ways to motivate my Maltese students to learn English and to become as enthusiastic about learning English as I was to teach them. I had already been teaching English to teenagers for over fifteen years. Throughout this time, I had striven to keep high my motivation to teach after so many years. It was obvious to me by now that my source of motivation or lack of it lay with my students. They were crucial in helping me to maintain the passion for my job. Consequently, I became interested in the issue of the relationship between teacher and student motivation, and what influences such a relationship.

Therefore, I decided to conduct a research study which sought to investigate the relationship between the motivation of secondary school teachers of English and their students. It involved students who were in their final years of compulsory schooling. Proficiency in English is not only crucial for them to be able to have a successful career but also for them to be fully functioning Maltese citizens. Malta is a bilingual country and Maltese is largely spoken solely on the island, therefore proficiency in English as the language of wider communication is indispensable. Since teacher and student motivation are key contributors to improving English language teaching and learning, it was deemed propitious to investigate the relationships that may exist between teacher and student motivation and what would enhance each.

The results of the investigation were based on a mixed-methods study conducted in twelve state secondary schools (eleven to sixteen years). It comprised 612 students (fifteen to sixteen years) along with thirty-seven teachers. Twelve of the latter were interviewed for the qualitative part of the study.

Consider the relationship between teachers and students. Which interacting factors do you think affect motivation?

The study revealed that the main factors impacting the relationship between teacher and student motivation are twofold:

1 Teacher–student rapport
   A good teacher–student rapport increased student motivation. A positive relationship puts students at ease and reduces their anxiety when learning and using English in the classroom. In such cases the teacher is accessible and personally involved in the students' learning. Teachers also claimed that the relationship they have with their students is the main motivating force for them to obtain increased satisfaction from their teaching. They enjoyed working with students and found student progress to be very rewarding.

2 Teacher self-efficacy
   Results revealed that an efficacious teacher heightens the students' desire to learn English. Self-efficacy is the belief that one is able to do one's job well and the perception that one is able to achieve professionally set goals (Bandura, 1997). It refers to the teacher's

belief that s/he can help students learn (Pintrich and Schunk, 2002). The literature on self-efficacy establishes clearly that factors such as the context in which they teach, class management and the feedback provided by significant others affect a teacher's self-efficacy. From the study in Malta it transpired that another factor in raising the level of a teacher's efficacy was the 'challenges offered by the job'.

How can teachers improve their teacher–student rapport and teacher efficacy?

Teacher participants from the study advised that teachers are to

- work on their qualities such as empathy, warmth and trustworthiness which would enhance their rapport with their students;
- be aware of their students' needs as students are more receptive when they feel that these are being met;
- work on their communication skills, both verbal and non-verbal. Students of different abilities and personalities may require a range of different communicative strategies and skills;
- follow CPD courses as these boost their self-efficacy. These could be on-going and offer support to discuss teacher stress and anxiety;
- seek professional feedback from various sources. Feedback might be translated into more effective and meaningful teaching practices;
- be provided with a centralized structure which deals with disruptive students, the necessary resources and a clean and pleasant school environment;
- be supported in their endeavour to promote autonomous learning so that they have more time for individual student attention; and
- be provided with opportunities for career improvement as an incentive for rendering their teaching more effective and efficient.

All the above can be made more possible by reducing teachers' in-class hours. This would enable teachers to offer their students more individual attention related to their subject, spend more time on preparation and on professional self-development.

Which of the above could you enact in your own teaching?

A personal reflection

Previous to my study there had essentially been only three studies which analysed the effectiveness of motivational strategies in language teachers in the classroom: (Dörnyei and Csizer (1998), Cheng and Dörnyei (2007) and Guilloteaux and Dörnyei (2008). My study showed that the major contributors to raising student motivation are the good relationship that teachers build with their students and their own teaching efficacy. This helped me to reflect on my own practice.

Such findings made me realize that I had managed to raise my students' motivation to learn by the approach that I adopted in class and the good relationship I had built with them. I made sure that I got to know the students enough to be able to choose the right topics and activities which triggered their interest. It was an endless search for effective ways of teaching to lure the students into the motivation 'web'. Enthusiasm in class, what Keller et al. (2014) refer to as 'dispositional teacher enthusiasm', directly correlated with the students' interest in the subject. The more they became motivated the more they looked forward to their English lessons with me. It also went beyond the classroom situation as students were looking for ways to improve their English so as to please me and also to be able to participate more fully in the class activities.

All this fed into my sense of teacher efficacy as I felt good about my own professional practice. In other words, it had turned into a cycle of the more I was able to motivate my students, the more I was motivated and enthusiastic about my teaching. This spurred me on to motivate them further.

This whole process is, of course, not that straightforward. Although I made sure that my rapport with my students was a good one, I still believe that the teacher has to maintain some professional distance and not become too friendly as this may give rise to class management issues. It is always best to have a professional relationship with the learners. In fact, the students soon came to realize that my main interest was for them to succeed in improving their level of English language proficiency and to be successful in life. The moment they were aware of this, they became more cooperative in class.

Can you identify what actions can be considered professional and what crosses the line into personal when working with students?

Teachers need to be aware of the intimate relationship that exists between their own motivation and that of their students. They need to recognize that just as their students' lack of motivation may adversely affect their teaching (Keller et al., 2014), their own attitudes and professional comportment may detract from the levels of enthusiasm and motivation of their students. It is a synergistic cycle for which teachers are largely responsible in view of their determinant role in the classroom situation. It is a responsibility that teachers cannot renounce when faced with unenthusiastic students. They should conceive this as an opportunity for them to renew their commitment to teaching and to their students. This would result in their revitalizing their teaching persona.

Further reading

Bandura, A. (1997) *Self-Efficacy: The Exercise of Control*, New York: W. H. Freeman.

Cheng, H., and Dörnyei, Z. (2007) 'The Use of Motivational Strategies in Language Instruction: The Case of EFL Teaching in Taiwan', *Innovation in Language Learning and Teaching*, 1, pp. 153–73.

Dörnyei, Z., and Csizér, K. (1998) 'Ten Commandments for Motivating Language Learners: Results of an Empirical Study', *Language Teaching Research*, 2, pp. 203–29.

Guilloteaux, M., and Dörnyei, Z. (2008) 'Motivating Language Learners: A Classroom-Oriented Investigation of the Effects of Motivational Strategies on Student Motivation', *TESOL Quarterly*, 42:1, pp. 55–77.

Keller, M., Goetz, T., Becker, E., Morger, V., and Hensley, L. (2014) 'Feeling and Showing: A New Conceptualisation of Dispositional Teacher Enthusiasm and Its Relationship to Students' Interest', *Learning and Instruction*, 33:1, pp. 29–38.

Mifsud, M. (2011) 'The Relationship of Teachers' and Students' Motivation in ELT in Malta: A Mixed Methods Study', published doctoral dissertation, University of Nottingham, UK.

Pintrich, P., and Schunk, D. (2002) *Motivation in Education: Theory, Research and Applications* (2nd ed.), New Jersey: Prentice Hall.

10

What social justice is being achieved through education?

Have assessment reforms in England brought about improvement or increased inequality?

Sue Hammond

Social justice is a ubiquitous international issue and perhaps a strange one to be considering in the context of a hitherto successful economy such as that of the UK. It has been argued that a prosperous economy benefits all citizens, yet some of the world's wealthiest countries have experienced growing inequalities in recent decades (Wilkinson and Pickett, 2009; OECD, 2014; UNESCO, 2016). Indeed, when Theresa May became Prime Minister in July 2016, she gave an impassioned speech about her party's commitment to eradicating the social injustices that exist across the UK (May, 2016). Yet, less than eighteen months later, four members of the government's Social

Mobility Commission resigned because of the lack of real action or progress in addressing inequalities between rich and poor.

In various reports on social mobility (e.g. Allen, 2011a), the education system has consistently been identified as a focus for tackling disparities between rich and poor and increasing opportunities for children from socially disadvantaged families. As education is managed separately in each of the countries that make up the UK, this chapter focuses on the structure of education policies in England and the possible impact on inequality.

Why is social inequality still a significant issue for education systems across the world?

Arguably the most influential change in English education policy came about in the year 2000 when the Labour government of the time introduced private sponsorship and the Academisation Policy into state education (HM government, 2000). A programme of 'free schools' and 'forced academisation' was unrelentingly pursued (Ball, 2013, p. 35). The involvement of private business and global managerial practices seems to have resulted in a data-driven approach to evaluating teaching, of what counts as learning or is valued as education (Ball, 2003, 2013). For academies, free schools and the remaining State schools, the drive to demonstrate children's progress has often been achieved by narrowing the curriculum, teaching to the test and a formulaic approach to learning. While the sponsors of many academy schools may be well intentioned, there has been no substantial evidence that such schools are significantly changing the life chances of children from low-income families (DfE, 2016b).

Why do you think this is?

This lack of achievement is despite the tight management of performance data and the narrow assessments on which it is based, or the considerable funding required to implement the policy. The Department for Education (DfE, 2016a) contends that 'Academy performance is monitored directly by regional school commissioners who intervene promptly in instances of underperformance'. Although such a statement raises the question of how 'underperformance' is measured, as well as about the funding directed at regional commissioners, it also highlights the issue of a lack of authentic school autonomy and the standardization of performance. Moreover, it directs the gaze of policymakers and policy implementers, including teachers, away from the lives of children growing up in poverty and the structural inequalities that perpetuate academic failure (Gorski, 2016). The 'structural inequality' central to this chapter is the structure of the discourse that characterizes English education policy.

Are there structures that appear to reproduce inequalities in your education system or are there policies or practices that have reduced inequality?

Discourse is a powerful aspect of language and language has an important role in the formulation of educational policies and practices. Discourse reaches beyond word choices to how words are appropriated in order to project images, views, prejudices and far more. It enables communities to define themselves, to identify who is or is not part of a particular cultural group. It can also be manipulated to denigrate or marginalize others (Gee, 2011). According to many social commentators and academics, there is a long history of discourse that portrays the 'other' as in need of saving, of having inferior social and cultural practices (Hobson, 1902; Bourdieu and Passeron, 1977; Said, 1978; González et al., 2005), or elevates certain groups and their social and cultural practices.

Success in speaking and writing in Standard English is part of the discourse that has come to define children's early performance in the English primary school system. The Spelling, Punctuation and Grammar (SPaG) summative tests introduced into primary schools by the government's Standards and Testing Agency in 2016 have high status. They matter to a school's success or failure, as well as to how individual children are perceived, and are a priority when planning the curriculum. Therefore, it might be argued that the structural ideology of the tests has added to the marginalization of children from socially disadvantaged families. They are the children least likely in their daily lives to be exposed to and immersed in the linguistic practices of Standard English. Those children for whom 'them ones', 'we done' or 'ain't got no' is part of their local dialect, and shaped by the rules of the vernacular grammar (Gee, 2011; Pinker, 2016), are immediately placed at a disadvantage when it comes to the testing regime. They have to acquire a new oral language or, at the very least, an understanding of a different formula for written language if they are to succeed in the institutional environment. They have to be able to 'code switch' between the familiar grammar and lexicon of home and the linguistic rules of the classroom (Heller, 1992). Though learning to communicate in traditional English offers advantages over time, struggling to meet the test requirements at aged six or seven and ten or eleven years can negatively affect children's well-being and sense of identity (Hammond, 2015). It may additionally lead to a model of education based on a deficit ideology (Gorski, 2016); that is, a view of what children cannot do rather than what they can.

What is the nature of the 'discourse' in your own education system?

The grammar test is neither founded on research evidence demonstrating its appropriateness for young children or its long-term educational benefits. Richard Hudson, Emeritus Professor of Linguistics at University College London (UCL) was a key advisor on the implementation of the statutory SPaG tests in England, alongside two other highly regarded university researchers, Ronald Carter and Debra Myhill, and Geoff Barton, a former Secondary English teacher. Hudson, in an interview with Mansell (2017) stated, 'We started off with the primary curriculum, which we were a bit unconfident about as none of us had much experience of primary education'. In 2017, while 77 per cent of children achieved the required 'standard' in the grammar, punctuation and spelling test (2017) there is no data on the effects this had on the breadth of the curriculum or children and teachers' motivation. There is anecdotal evidence to suggest that children in some of the poorest communities receive the most restricted curricula because of the pressure to meet national standards. Group interviews with Post Graduate Teaching Training students at a university in the south of England include the following statement:

> There isn't time to do Art or Music, or History and Geography, or even much Science. We have to raise our results and this means concentrating on English and maths.

Is it possible to eradicate inequalities by providing children with a curriculum based on the cultural and social practices of their wealthier peers?

While social and 'material inequalities' (Dahlberg and Moss, 2005, p. 41; see also, Ritzer, 2010; Wilkinson and Pickett, 2010; Lambirth, 2010) continue to exist, it may seem as though there is little that can be done to overcome inequalities. Perhaps removing some of the barriers perpetuated through educational discourse could lead to a broader, more complex view of socially disadvantaged children and the sort of exciting school experiences that equip them with knowledge of the world around them. If we are committed to social mobility, perhaps we need a new vision for schooling that is open to all voices.

In what ways could schools help to overcome the inequalities of birth?

Further reading

Allen, G. (2011a) *Early Intervention: The Next Steps. An Independent Report to Her Majesty's Government*, London: Cabinet Office.

Ball, S. (2003) 'The Teacher's Soul and the Terrors of Performativity', *Journal of Education Policy*, 18:2, pp. 215–28.

Ball, S. (2013) *Education, Justice and Democracy: The Struggle over Ignorance and Opportunity*. The Centre for Labour and Social Studies (Class).

Bourdieu, P., and Passeron, J.-C. (1977) *Reproduction in Education, Society and Culture*, London: Sage.

Dahlberg, G., and Moss, P. (2005) *Ethics and Politics in Early Childhood Education*, Abingdon: Routledge Falmer.

Department for Education (DfE) (2016a) *10 Facts You Need to Know about Academies*. Available at: https://www.gov.uk/government/news/10-facts-you-need-to-know-about-academies (Accessed December 2017).

Department for Education (DfE) (2016b) *Statistical Working Paper: Multi-academy Trust Performance Measures: England, 2014 to 2015*. Available at: https://www.gov.uk/government/uploads/system/uploads/attachment_data/file/535604/SFR32_2016_text.pdf (Accessed December 2017).

Gee, J. (2011) *How to Do Discourse Analysis: A Toolkit*, London: Routledge.

González, N., Moll, L., and Amanti, C. (2005). *Funds of Knowledge: Theorizing Practices in Households, Communities, and Classrooms*, New Jersey: Lawrence Erlbaum Associates

Gorski, P. (2016) 'Poverty and the Ideological Imperative', *Journal of Education for Teaching*, 42:4, pp. 378–86.

Hammond, S. (2015) 'Beyond the Image: Revealing the Texts of Young Children's Lives', Unpublished Doctoral thesis, Canterbury Christ Church University.

Heller, M. (1992) 'The Politics of Codeswitching and Language Choice', *Journal of Multilingual and Multicultural Development*, 13:1–2, pp. 123–42.

Her Majesty's Government (HM) (2000) *Learning and Skills Act*. Available at: http://www.legislation.gov.uk/ukpga/2000/21/contents (Accessed December 2017).

Hobson, J. (1902) *Imperialism: A Study*, New York: James Pott.

Lambirth, A. (2010) 'Class Consciousness, Power, Identity, and the Motivation to Teach', *Power and Education*, 2, pp. 209–22.

Mansell, W. (2017) Battle on the Adverbials Front: Grammar Advisers Raise Worries about Sats Tests and Teaching. *Guardian*, 9 May 2017. Available at: https://www.theguardian.com/education/2017/may/09/fronted-adverbials-sats-grammar-test-primary (Accessed January 2018).

May, T. (2016) Speech https://www.gov.uk/government/speeches/statement-from-the-new-prime-minister-theresa-may (Accessed December 2017).

OECD (2014) *Inequality Hurts Economic Growth, Finds OECD Research.* Available at: http://www.oecd.org/newsroom/inequality-hurts-economic-growth.htm (Accessed January 2018).

Pinker, S. (2016) *Word of Mouth*, Radio 4, 5 April 2016. Available at: http://www.bbc.co.uk/programmes/b075pz7x (Accessed January 2018).

Ritzer, G. (2010) *Globalization: A Basic Text*, Chichester: Wiley-Blackwell.

Said, E. (1978) *Orientalism*, New York: Pantheon Books.

Standards and Testing Agency (STA) Key stage 2 tests: 2016 English grammar, punctuation and spelling test materials. Available at: https://www.gov.uk/government/publications/key-stage-2-tests-2016-english-grammar-punctuation-and-spelling-test-materials (Accessed January 2018).

UNESCO (2016) *World Social Science Report, 2016: Challenging Inequalities; Pathways to a Just World*, UNESCO.

Wilkinson, R., and Pickett, K. (2009) *The Spirit Level: Why More Equal Societies Almost Always Do Better*, London: Penguin.

11

What pedagogical questions are raised in reforming early literacy instruction?

Exploring the tension between government expectations and broader child development beliefs in Norway

Mona E. Flognfeldt, Eva Michaelsen and Kirsten Palm

In Norway, children start primary school at the age of six. Kindergartens aim to foster children's self-esteem and childhoods where well-being, friendship and play are central. Kindergarten activities include language stimulation and language play. However, from the first year of primary school, children's emergent functional literacy is a pedagogical priority in the school language, Norwegian, and their first foreign language, English. Learners' conceptual and lexical development is seen as an important first step towards literacy. A central consideration for this chapter is whether children are ready to benefit from formal schooling at the age of six. Is the compulsory screening of young learners' reading skills conducive to learning, or does it take away time from creative and educative activities? Further deliberation is given to language-minority learners and whether they have equal opportunities for deep learning.

Are six-year-olds ready for primary school, or are schools suited to their needs?

For more than 250 years, children in Norway started school at the age of seven. In 1997, school-starting age was lowered to six. This reform met with quite a lot of resistance from primary and pre-school teachers and a compromise was made to combine the best from kindergarten and school. The intention was that the first year of schooling would be characterized by play and a playful approach to emergent literacy development. However, even before the reform was implemented, international tests like PISA[1] (OECD, 2018), TIMMS and PIRLS[2] (IEA, 2018) impacted on educational priorities. When results from international tests and national achievement tests did not meet expectations, a shift took place towards more traditional instructional methods from the first grade (age six). The number of lessons per week increased to the point where, in many schools, six- and seven-year-olds had 90-minute lessons without a real break outside the classroom. This is despite considerable evidence that breaks are vital for the youngest learners (Pellegrini, 2009; Vingdal, 2018), for whom attention will increase if they are given sufficient pauses between intensive periods of classroom work.

1   OECD Programme for International Student Assessment (PISA) is a triennial international survey, which aims to evaluate education systems worldwide by testing the skills and knowledge of fifteen-year-old students: http://www.oecd.org/pisa/aboutpisa/
2   IEA's TIMSS & PIRLS International Study Center conducts regular international comparative assessments of student achievement in mathematics and science (TIMSS) and in reading (PIRLS) in more than sixty countries.

Critical voices among teachers and researchers question whether today's schools accommodate the youngest learners' needs. Arguably, a more holistic view of the pupils is necessary, identifying their cognitive, emotional and social needs as an integral part of their learning process (Klitmøller and Sommer, 2016). Very young learners can be seen as *learning bodies* whereby functional aspects of their physical, cognitive, emotional, social and motor development interact and influence each other. However, the traditional orientation of schools has been theoretical-cognitive, separating body and cognition (Vingdal, 2018).

Is this the best way to stimulate young learners?

The role of play in school, 'play as learning' versus 'play as pedagogy', is being debated internationally. Playful and experimental approaches to learning in the first few primary years are recommended by many early childhood experts (e.g Hunter and Walsh, 2014). However, despite their apparent importance for children's development and future learning, little space is currently devoted to these approaches in Norwegian schools.

Other international forces influencing Norwegian education have been the World Bank and the OECD. The national curricula now contain *learning outcomes* from the very start in all school subjects, and there has been an increased focus on the training of basic skills from kindergarten or early primary school.

Do we need a universal approach to education in early childhood?

Early intervention has become a ubiquitous catchphrase in education. Early interventions are meant to prevent dropout from school. In the initial primary years, this means early recognition of pupils who struggle, a call for differentiated instruction and closer follow-up of learners. A targeted group is language-minority children who do not speak Norwegian well enough to follow grade-level curricular activities (Norway, Ministry of Education and Research, 2017). However, playful learning and ideas about *how* instruction for early intervention should be enacted are not mentioned in policy documents. So, it seems that the solution offered is more of the same traditional ways of teaching and practising the language. Klitmøller and Sommer (2016) argue that if early intervention means starting even earlier with school-oriented learning at the cost of play, it will have detrimental rather than beneficial effects. Children will get tired of learning even before they start school, they will lose interest in subjects and become restless (Palm et al., 2018).

Do young children tire of learning or the approaches that are used in formal education?

What are the benefits and challenges of screening primary learners' reading skills? The so-called 'PISA shock' in 2000 became a stepping-stone for reforming compulsory education in Norway. In reading, Norway was number thirteen among the thirty-one OECD countries (Lie et al., 2001). In the evaluation of the 1997 school reform (Klette, 2003), researchers observed that teachers were not good at communicating their expectations clearly to their pupils. There was little specific advice on how learners could improve. During the ensuing years, screening tests in reading literacy were developed to obtain quality information about pupils' achievements. The purpose was to identify the 20 per cent with the least developed skills in order to act early and support pupils with reading difficulties.

Reading tests in years one, two and three became compulsory and carried out across the country in April each year. There is no doubt that teachers' knowledge of individual pupils' reading development is crucial information. However, during the first years of this testing, results were published in the newspapers, and schools began to compete to have the fewest pupils below the 20 per cent benchmark. This was not the purpose of the screening tests. Teachers at further-education (CPD) courses have expressed that one outcome was stressed teachers who wanted their pupils to perform well. The teachers also witnessed stressed pupils afraid of failing. Competition-oriented discourse accompanied these tests from the beginning, and the weight on performance rather than learning may have overshadowed any good intentions. While the importance of creativity and deep learning in school is emphasized in the Main Curriculum Section – foundational values and principles in basic education (Norway. Government, 2017), there are potential challenges in managing these at the same time as offering the reading tuition required for the tests.

In the standardized screening, the pupils complete the test on their own, only guided by the teacher's oral instruction. They are not allowed to ask for help, because this will compromise the assessment (finding the 20 per cent lowest achievers in order to intervene early and support them in their reading development). If teachers are uncertain about a pupil's results, they may use the screening test in a *dynamic* way (Sternberg and Grigorenko, 2002). This entails supporting the pupils when doing the tasks, in order to find out if a given pupil simply had a bad day or was distracted during the instruction. Several dynamic tools have been launched to monitor pupils' reading skills, but one case study (Michaelsen, 2018) revealed that teachers found it difficult to utilize the knowledge obtained well enough to plan and enact it in their teaching. Nevertheless, used by competent teachers these tools could be implemented in everyday tuition and replace the standardized screening tests. Today, many teachers feel obliged to teach to the standardized test. Can the use of dynamic tools free up time to ensure a more creative learning environment?

Do all learners have an optimal learning environment?

As a result of migration and globalization, many primary classrooms in Norway are multilingual and multicultural. Pupils learn Norwegian and English from the start, but learners from language-minority backgrounds are not always offered equitable opportunities to build on their previous language experience. The language through which emergent multilingual children are socialized and have started their conceptual development is not welcomed in many diverse classrooms (Chumak-Horbatsch, 2012). Some schools in fact have a policy of 'Norwegian only', an assimilative rather than inclusive orientation which may negatively affect pupils' acquisition of English. If deep learning for all is an overall ambition and educational aim, how can this practice be justified as equitable, if only some of the pupils are encouraged to make direct links between the new language and their mother tongue? According to curricular aims, they are all expected to look for similarities between English and their home languages. The official and the *practised* subject curricula seem to be at odds with each other (Young, 2018). This policy can have a potentially detrimental effect on young learners' identity development and lead to a disempowering loss of their first language proficiency. A further and more general infelicitous effect may be that they will struggle to access academic content in other school subjects. Moreover, it raises questions about whether the alleged cognitive and linguistic benefits of being multilingual can be realized in a predominantly monolingual pedagogical orientation (Bialystok and Craik, 2010; Cenoz and Gorter, 2011; Jessner, 2018).

The situation in Norway is not unique (Conteh, 2012; De Angelis, 2015). An important question is whether the drive for social cohesion is perceived locally as more important than ensuring optimal learning conditions for the development of every child's functional literacy. Teachers may not be familiar with multilingualism and the nature of multilingual learning. It appears that it is up to teachers themselves on how to use multilingualism as a resource (Palm, 2018). Their teacher education may not have prepared them well enough to help *all* learners benefit from the affordances of the multilingual classroom. To facilitate every pupil's literacy development, an increased focus on teachers' multilingual awareness is called for (Flognfeldt, 2018).

What would be vital features of this kind of professional competence?

Further reading

Bialystok, E., and Craik, F. I. M. (2010) 'Cognitive and Linguistic Processing in the Bilingual Mind', *Current Directions in Psychological Science*, 191, pp. 19–23.

Cenoz, J., and Gorter, D. (2011) 'Focus on Multilingualism: A Study of Trilingual Writing', *The Modern Language Journal*, 95 (iii), pp. 356–69.

Chumak-Horbatsch, R. (2012) *Linguistically Appropriate Practice*, Toronto: University of Toronto Press.

Conteh, J. (2012) 'Families, Pupils and Teachers Learning Together in a Multilingual British City', *Journal of Multilingual and Multicultural Development*, 331, pp. 101–16.

De Angelis, G. (2015) 'English L3 Learning in a Multilingual Context: The Role of Parental Education and L2 Exposure with the Living Community', *International Journal of Multilingualism*, 12:4, pp. 435–52.

Flognfeldt, M. (2018) 'Teaching and Learning English in Multilingual Early Primary Classrooms', in Michaelsen, E., and Palm, K. (eds), *Den viktige begynneropplæringa – En forskningsbasert tilnærming*, Oslo: Universitetsforlaget.

Hunter, T., and Walsh, G. (2014) 'From Policy to Practice? The Reality of Play in Primary School Classes in Northern Ireland', *International Journal of Early Years Education*, 22, pp. 19–37.

IEA (2018) 'TIMSS & PIRLS International Study Center. Assessments of Student Achievement in Mathematics and Science (TIMSS) and in Reading (PIRLS)' [Online]. Available at: https://timssandpirls.bc.edu/about.html (Accessed February 2018).

Jessner, U. (2018) 'Language Awareness in Multilingual Learning and Teaching', in Garrett, P., and Cots, J. M. (eds), *The Routledge Handbook of Language Awareness*, New York: Routledge, pp. 257–74.

Klette, K. (ed.) (2003) *Klasserommets praksisformer etter Reform 97*, Oslo: Pedagogisk forskningsinstitutt, Universitetet i Oslo.

Klitmøller, J., and Sommer, D. (2016) 'Turboladet globalisering og den fremtidsparate skole – en vision', *Nordisk tidsskrift for pedagogikk og kritikk*,

pp. 3–19. Available at: https://pedagogikkogkritikk.no/index.php/ntpk/
article/view/437#CIT0041_437 (Accessed February 2018).

Lie, S., Kjærnsli, M., Roe, A., and Turmo, A. (2001) *Godt rustet for framtida?
Norske 15-åringers kompetanse i lesing og realfag i et internasjonalt
perspektiv.* [Well prepared for the future? Norwegian 15-year-olds'
competence in reading and scientific subjects in an international
perspective]. Oslo: Institutt for lærerutdanning og skoleutvikling,
Universitetet i Oslo.

Michaelsen, E. (2018) 'Dynamisk kartlegging av leseutvikling', in Michaelsen,
E., and Palm, K. (eds), *Den viktige begynneropplæringa – En forskningsbasert
tilnærming*, Oslo: Universitetsforlaget.

Norway Government (2017) *Overordnet del – verdier og prinsipper for
grunnopplæringen* [Main curriculum Section – foundational values and
principles in basic education] Available at: https://www.regjeringen.no/cont
entassets/37f2f7e1850046a0a3f676fd45851384/overordnet-del---verdier-og-
prinsipper-for-grunnopplaringen.pdf (Accessed February 2018).

Norway Ministry of Education and Research (2017) *Lærelyst – tidlig
innsats og kvalitet i skolen* [Eagerness to learn – early intervention
and quality in education]. Meld. St. [White paper] 21 (2016–17).
Oslo: Kunnskapsdepartementet.

OECD (2018) Programme for International Student Assessment
(PISA) Available at: http://www.oecd.org/pisa/aboutpisa/ (Accessed
February 2018).

Palm, K. (2018) 'Enspråklig begynneropplæring i flerspråklige klasserom?', in
Michaelsen, E., and Palm, K. (eds), *Den viktige begynneropplæringa – En
forskningsbasert tilnærming*, Oslo: Universitetsforlaget.

Palm, K., Becher, A. A., and Michaelsen, E. (2018) 'Den viktige
begynneropplæringa – aktuelle fagområder og kritiske perspektiver', in
Michaelsen, E., and Palm, K. (eds), *Den viktige begynneropplæringa – En
forskningsbasert tilnærming*, Oslo: Universitetsforlaget.

Pellegrini, A. D. (2009). *The Role of Play in Human Development*, Oxford:
Oxford University Press.

Sternberg, R. J., and Grigorenko, E. L. (2002) *Dynamic Testing*, Cambridge:
Cambridge University Press.

Vingdal, I. M. (2018) 'Lærande kropp i endring', in Michaelsen, E., and Palm,
K. (eds), *Den viktige begynneropplæringa – En forskningsbasert tilnærming.*
Oslo: Universitetsforlaget.

Young, A. S. (2018) 'Language Awareness, Language Diversity and Migrant
Languages in the Primary School', in Garrett, P., and Cots, J. M. (eds),
The Routledge Handbook of Language Awareness, New York: Routledge,
pp. 23–39.

12

Does collaborative teaching practice work?

The opportunities and challenges of educational change in teacher education in Nepal

Tika Ram Pokhrel

Theory and practice are considered as two sides of a coin in teacher education programmes. The reason for balancing both can be justified, as prospective teachers are required to enhance their level of thinking as well as develop skills for instructional purposes. Making a strong connection between theory and practice is one of the major concerns of the professionals working on pre-service teacher education programmes in many parts of the world. Although some students fail to appreciate the reciprocal relationship between practical and academic components, there are several options for making such connections. Method courses are moderately helpful in achieving this (Unver, 2014), but combining practical teaching, practicum and internship courses seems to be the most successful approach in Nepal. This begins as a practical course work requirement, rather than volunteering work. Though different Nepalese universities use different terms when students go into school, including Practice Teaching, Internship and Practicum, the core aim is universal: that of moving students to realize how they are applying theory to practice and using practice to reflect on theory that will enhance it.

Fostering the professional development of Pre-service Teachers (PTs) is the main crux of school internship (Chennat, 2014). Furthermore, internship should lead students to the development of a broad repertoire of perspectives, professional capacities, teacher sensibilities and skills (Chennat, 2014). Through thinking, feeling and doing, internship programmes help future teachers widen their horizons, empowering them to manage real classroom situations. Internship is valued for the contribution it makes to students' success as teachers (Utah Valley University, n.d.). It is one of the twelve types of experiential learning (University of Tennessee, n.d.). In the Nepalese context, teacher education encompasses teaching skills, pedagogical theory and professional skills (National Campaign for Education, Nepal, 2017); during internships students are expected to master these in the social setting of schools.

Teaching practice in Nepal is considered one of the most powerful experiential learning platforms for prospective teachers and is the backbone of programmes at the Faculty of Education at Tribhuvan University (TU) (Archarya, 2017). The general framework of teaching practice can be summarized as preparation at the university followed by an extended clinical experience, of supervised practicum and student teaching opportunities, at least twenty-four to thirty-six weeks long (Oberg, 2001; Hébert, 2001; Glickman, 2001, Weiner, 2001; McCall, 2001, as cited in the National Campaign for Education Nepal, 2017, p. 15).

Practice Teaching in the university is carried out in three phases: orientation, microteaching and classroom teaching. After completing the application process, students receive general orientation information and then engage in two weeks' collaborative microteaching. They prepare lesson plans and teach each other, supported by an internal supervisor who also evaluates their microteaching. Each student is expected to deliver five short micro-lessons before they are assigned to schools for six weeks of actual classroom teaching.

What are the benefits and drawbacks of microteaching?

The major intent of the Practice Teaching programme is to give student teachers a tangible classroom teaching experience so that they can develop the required skills for their professional teaching after graduation (Gautam, n.d.). The duration of the practice varies between four and six weeks, depending on the programme level. However, it is argued that this must be more than just preparation of formal classroom skills and PTs as scholars in the teacher education programme need to play a role as change agents. There are two major concern in this chapter: to explore the possibilities of preparing PTs as change agents, and to discuss the design of internships aimed at integrating classroom theory with practical work experience in every day work situations. Both strands are based on the premise that learning in the work world can enhance learning in the university and action in the community. The internship programme provides students with an avenue to expand knowledge and skills as well as to contribute to the activities being undertaken by the organization.

To what extent is theory overtly applied to practice in your experience?

The existing practices of internship, or practice teaching, in Nepal can be summarized in four levels, each with corresponding challenges and opportunities:

Level I: Personal level collaboration

In this level of collaboration, teaching practice is controlled by the evaluation system. This is the dominant practice in Nepal. For example, at some universities, microteaching consists of 20 per cent and is evaluated by the Campus Supervisor (CS). Actual teaching consists of 80 per cent and is evaluated by the School Supervisor (SS), the Internal Supervisor (IS) and the External Supervisor (ES). This indicates that teaching practice is maybe less focused on developmental aspects and more on judgemental aspects. The SS is a schoolteacher who usually teaches the subject assigned to the PT and mentors the PT in school regarding classroom teaching and learning processes. The university teacher, the IS, supervises performance and provides feedback. The CS is a college/university teacher, who is especially responsible for grading microteaching. The same person can be CS as well as IS. The ES is the final evaluator from the university and he/she works as an independent evaluator.

This is an efficient model when there are institutional resource constraints, such as a CS needing to work with many PTs. During the teaching practice the PT prepares plans and delivers lessons independently. Sometimes, a SS and an Internal Supervisor observe certain lessons and provide feedback for further improvement. There are several challenges, most of which are linked with the quality of professional development. For example, in some cases, the observation and feedback by SS and IS becomes just a formality. Furthermore, Gautam (n d.) mentions that IS supervision can be limited. There may be little or poor quality feedback, incomplete lesson observations or the schools might use the PTs as extra teachers, requiring them to teach any class which is vacant. At this stage, the PTs probably have limited classroom management skills. Thus, the major challenge is collaboration between PT, SS and IS, while each of them are trying to fulfil their separate requirements.

With the good quality direction that some PTs receive from their supervisor, they gain in confidence to teach and to deal with student behaviours in the class. Additionally, in some cases PTs bring teaching materials and motivate students to learn. In many cases though, six week Practice Teaching/Internship programmes run in a completely formal way. The conflict of interest can be sensed in both the schools and universities or colleges involved. There are apparent challenges with the existing practice and internship models and the transference of skills (National Campaign for Education, Nepal, 2017, p. 18).

As a result of the formality and conflicts of interest, many school authorities do not accept student teachers to practise at their schools. Among the reasons are: they are less qualified, the practice is too short, students do not take the lessons seriously or lack of consistent teaching. Though these do present challenges, there are positive innovations that student teachers can bring (Subedi, 2009, p. 138).

Level II: Group level collaboration

When the College Supervisor plays an active role in supporting PTs and other colleagues try to resolve challenges collaboratively (CS, SS and PT), things work better. To this end, the PTs are prepared for different aspects of school life, such as planning, delivery and building supportive relationships with teachers and other school colleagues. PTs observe lessons delivered by the respective teachers in the schools. PTs and teachers discuss the lessons and share ideas. Then they plan and deliver lessons together, discussing the successful parts and areas to improve after the class. Finally, PTs plan the lessons and the teachers go through the plans and suggest any modifications. The teachers observe the PT's classes and give feedback. Similarly, college or university IS observe classes and record PT's classroom teaching throughout the session (Subedi, 2009). When they then discuss the student's progress collaboratively, learning opportunities can transpire. As the alliance is not formal, it is hard to form collaborative groups and, even when formed, the collaboration may not last.

Level III: Organizational level collaboration

Teacher training colleges and universities collaborate in order to bring synergy to their teaching practices. They develop models for conducting practice teaching for either organization. One organization hosts the students of another university and arranges teaching placements, with the host organization taking responsibility for evaluating students' teaching. For example, TU Nepal host PTs from HiOA (now Oslo Metropolitan University), Norway, in their practice abroad programme. The host institute assigns supervisors who work in the respective schools guided by negotiated guidelines provided by HiOA. For students and supervisors, the programme provides a form of third-party evaluation: students learn to work in a different culture and accommodate different ways of learning. They gain wider experiences through teaching and sharing idea with teachers. Supervisors also gain fresh insights into the process of learning. The major challenge of such collaboration lies within the conflicting systems of the two institutions. For example, teaching six full days of lessons has been a totally new experience, with many challenges, for the Norwegian students visiting Nepal.

What are the most powerful lessons students learn from a teaching practice in another country?

Level IV: Social level collaboration

When practice teaching or internship is considered as an opportunity to initiate change in schools' traditional practices, a high level of social collaboration is needed. At Level IV, students are motivated and ready to contribute to existing pedagogical processes. When the leadership provides a vehicle for authentic partnerships and collective agency, the social level of collaboration can be transformative (Reicher, Haslam and Hopkins, 2005).

The main intent of social level collaboration is for students to work with stakeholders from schools, communities and universities to implement a plan. For example, in one internship programme the students initiated a transformation in the education of a rural village in Nepal.[1] They were motivated to explore different options to bring tangible changes, such as using activity-based learning instead of traditional methods of instruction. This was a collaborative level of internship in which students learnt from the teachers and community people and had the opportunity to test their ideas. Perhaps because they were prepared to listen and to learn rather than simply implementing new approaches, the students began to win the trust of the local people. All the groups involved were able to explore possibilities for developing different types of learning projects through authentically collaborative relationships. The parents and other community members shared their cultural practices and embraced opportunities to learn from the student teachers.

What types of productive collaboration could students carry out in school?

The main intent of the levels are to share practices of teaching in Nepal. These levels are created with a view to collaboration and each has opportunities and challenges. A college or university can opt into more than one level of collaboration in a teaching practice, offering unique opportunities for different groups of students and the communities in which they teach.

Further reading

Acharya, K. (2016) 'Teaching Practice at Tribhuvan University', unpublished conference paper at International Conference, HIOA, Norway.
Chennat, S. (2014) 'Internship in Pre-service Teacher Education Programme: A Global Perspective', *International Journal of Research in Applied and Social Sciences*, 2:11, pp. 79–94.
Gautam, Ganga Ram (n.d.) *Practice Teaching: A Reflection* NELTA Choutari.

1   (A glimpse of activities is given in YouTube at https://www.youtube.com/watch?v=SxTGhlewd RU&t=38s).

Howe, A., and Stubbs, H. (1996) 'Empowering Science Teachers: A Model for Professional Development', *Journal of Science Teacher Education*, 3, pp. 167–82.

National Campaign for Education Nepal (2017) *Pre-service Teacher Education in Nepal: A Qualitative Case Study.*

Reicher, S., Haslam, S., and Hopkins, N. (2005) 'Social Identity and the Dynamics of Leadership: Leaders and Followers as Collaborative Agents in the Transformation of Social Reality', *Leadership Quarterly*, 16:4, pp. 547–68.

Subedi, D. (2009) 'Assessing English Language Teaching Student Teachers on Teaching Practice', *Journal of NELTA*, XIV:1–2, pp. 138–45.

The University of Tennessee. *Experience Learning* (n.d.) available at: https://experiencelearning.utk.edu/types/.

Unver, G. (2014) 'Connecting Theory and Practice in Teacher Education: A Case Study', *Educational Sciences: Theory & Practice*, 14:4, pp. 1402–7.

Utah Valley University. *Secondary Education* (n.d.) Available at https://www.uvu.edu/education/secondary/student_teaching/student_internship.html. https://www.uvu.edu/education/secondary/studentteaching.html. Accessed November 2018.

Vocabulary.com (n.d.) Available at: https://www.vocabulary.com/dictionary/internship.

13

How can we learn from teaching in another country?

A different model on which to draw to improve education in Tanzania

Alison Leonard

In this chapter the reflections of four Tanzanian teachers about practices in the United Kingdom (UK) and Tanzanian schools are used to challenge the hegemony that 'West knows best' (Quist-Adade and van Wyk, 2007). The Tanzanian teachers who visited the UK have senior management roles at a rural secondary day/boarding school with a specialist unit for visually impaired students. The school provides an inclusive education to over six hundred students. It aspires to

- ensure that class sizes are less than forty-five students;
- provide class sets of government-approved textbooks with Braille versions for its blind and visually impaired students; and
- improve academic performance in Tanzanian National Examinations. Students sit these exams at the ages of fourteen, sixteen and eighteen (NECTA, accessed 2017).

Two groups of Tanzanian teachers have visited the UK to support the school's link with its British Council Connecting Classrooms UK partner (British Council, 2017), and the UK school's Deputy Head teacher made a visit to Tanzania in 2015. Visits by teachers from the global south to the global north are rare (Leonard, 2014). During an exchange visit in 2017, the Tanzanian teachers were able to observe in a range of UK educational establishments: secondary and primary schools, specialist schools, a sixth-form academy and a university. Despite many differences between Tanzania and the UK, the teachers' reflections suggest that teachers, assistants, laboratory technicians and school management teams face similar issues. Therefore, three issues are discussed here, those of engaging students, provision for students with Special Educational Needs and the effective use of data. These are discussed within the context of science teaching.

Engaging students

Teacher K and his Head of Department, Teacher B, who was a biologist, were keen to learn about ways in which teachers stimulate young people's enthusiasm for science. They were especially interested in finding out how using experiments might support student engagement with theoretical knowledge:

> As teachers we all struggle to make the students be pro-active, be ready to study, to learn. And, it is like we have stubborn students here, some of the students [in the UK] also are stubborn. So the role of the teacher is to make these students study, or learn to their best. And yes, as teachers, we face challenges which are more likely the same. (Teacher B)

The reasons why science students in the UK and Tanzania can be 'stubborn' may be similar. If a young person is disinterested in the learning process, or the prescribed content, their teachers face similar challenges. In order to discover what lies behind students' barriers to learning, an apparent lack of motivation and to then engage disaffected students requires time and determination. Nevertheless, encouraging students to be ready to study and to learn are essential aspects of a teacher's daily routine, regardless of the subject taught or their length of service.

The reasons why a UK student is not engaged in a science lesson might differ to those of a Tanzanian student's, but both may be culturally driven. For example, in Tanzania a female student could be unwilling to question a male teacher, or a male peer's scientific explanation, or to be assertive.

Although in the UK there appear to be culturally different attitudes, there still may be underlying gender issues which impact on the motivation of female students. Campaigns in the UK to persuade girls to specialize in Science, Technology, Engineering and Mathematics (STEM) subjects are testament to the under-representation of girls in these subjects. This is of particular concern in Higher Education (Coughlan, 2015). A television documentary series investigating gender stereotypical attitudes in children as young as seven years of age has attempted to bring this issue to the attention of a wider UK public (Hoyle, 2017). Concerned about the waste of potential STEM talent, Dr Javid Abdelmoneim a researcher and physician working for Médecins Sans Frontières (MSF), conducted a controlled experiment in which he challenged gender stereotypes in a primary school. Over a six-week period, he was able to convince girls that they could succeed to the same level as boys, raising their self-esteem and enabling the boys to think differently too.

Challenging traditional views and attitudes that foster gender inequalities is common to the UK and Tanzania. There are indications that many behaviours and expectations are culturally embedded, but it is important that girls are persuaded that they can succeed in STEM subjects and should continue to study science alongside their male peers. While the Tanzanian teachers did not find simple answers to this issue during their visit, it did provide a forum for debating strategies and the changes that might be brought about by, for example, the language that is used to describe males and females.

Why does the challenge of gender stereotyping persist?

SEND provision

> We have our major challenge in the language of instruction: it is more of a barrier, it might not be a problem, particularly as in most of the classes most of the families are from the English speaking families, something like that in Gainsborough. (Teacher B)

English as the language of instruction is a global issue and the belief that it acts as a barrier to learning is not unique to Teacher B's students. Tanzanian secondary schooling is in English, which is a second or third language for most teachers and students. Teacher B noted similar challenges in UK. He visited a UK primary school in which students with English as an Additional Language (EAL) benefited from support from assistants able to offer tailored EAL provision:

There are students with different languages, who are from a different culture. Therefore they can struggle. So, yes the teachers are struggling, but because they have those assistants in the class then it is able. (Teacher B)

Many students in UK and Tanzanian schools struggle to cope with learning science in a second language (or even a third or fourth). This common difficulty was something Teacher B had not been aware of prior to his UK visit:

While a teacher teaches in a class, there is an assistant, of which here [Tanzania], we are not doing it thoroughly; we do it occasionally. Yes? Because of the number of staff and the time we have to do that. So, we are doing that, but not as effectively as our fellows are doing. But, again, the other thing that teachers do here but also in the UK they do, is about, to make sure that all the things that students are learning they help other students to interact with; for instance exams, notes and the other materials for teaching and learning.

Although teaching assistants were considered by the Tanzanian teachers to provide enormous benefits for UK students with EAL and other specific needs, the funding of assistants has been threatened by spending cuts affecting schools in England. SEND support in English secondary schools is already compromised (Tirraoro, 2016). In Tanzania, government commitments to resource and staff the Tanzanian school's Visual Impairment unit are yet to be realized.

Why is SEND provision a low priority in both countries?

The Effective Use of Data

The final issue that became evident through the visit was the effective use of data. Teacher C, who had a shared responsibility for monitoring and reporting students' academic progress in the Tanzanian school, identified some similarities in practice:

So we found the same things being done there. So, they are doing analysis of test results; they are allocating teaching periods to teachers; yeah? And some things like that. We found many things in common they are doing in a more advanced way than us. It is not quite different; I like to use the [phrase] 'advanced way'. (Teacher C)

UK schools use a variety of different ways to ensure that effective learning and teaching take place. These include formal lesson observations, 'learning walks' (for which senior management drop in to observe classes), book checks when the regularity and nature of teachers' marking are examined and regular formal assessments of students' work across a year group. Second, marking and moderation have also become norms in the education system of the UK, to ensure teachers' assessments and grading of their students' work is similar to that of other teachers. The time-pressures on Tanzanian teachers teaching large classes with limited resources pose a real challenge to maintaining marking and moderation of students' work.

When Teacher C mentioned the 'advanced' way that data was managed in UK schools, he was referring to the use of technology to monitor student and teacher attendance. Inconsistent teacher attendance and ensuring lessons are conducted in English are professional challenges unlikely to be encountered in UK schools. Teachers' professionalism can be promoted more effectively when schools have accurate data about teachers' classroom attendance and can nurture good quality in teaching. Though poor student attendance can be an issue for some UK schools, improving staff access to student data to address attendance and academic progress issues is something the Tanzanian school continues to work to address. Without accurate data about student attendance, teachers are unable to monitor the topics individuals have covered or manage pastoral issues. When school personnel have correct data about student punctuality, absenteeism and academic progress ways of addressing concerns can be more consistent and effective.

How can school data be utilized to greatest effect?

There were critical reflections that provided some potent revelations for the visiting teachers. For Teacher K, the school's Deputy Head teacher and a chemistry teacher, recognizing that his classroom practice was similar to that of his UK colleagues was empowering:

> One, which I can remember is about lesson preparation. It is almost the same [as] the way that we prepare our lessons here, it is almost the same as they do … I have noted that the way they, of course especially in the Science subjects, the way they do practicals: it is almost the same. There is not much difference between what we are doing and what they are doing. (Teacher K)

These reflections of four Tanzanian teachers offer us a small insight into comparative practices. Is it that 'West knows best' or are there other factors involved in the different status that may be attributed to individual education systems? While each Tanzanian teacher intends to implement ideas from educational practices seen in UK, it should not be assumed that such approaches are easily transferrable or will be received in the same way in another context.

From the comments of the teachers, what do you think are the underlying issues that affect how the education system in Tanzania and your own country operate?

Further reading

British Council. *Connecting Classrooms*. Available at: https://schoolsonline.britishcouncil.org/about-programmes/connecting-classrooms (Accessed November 2017).

Coughlan, S. (2015) 'Clever Girls Lack Confidence in Science and Maths'. Available at: http://www.bbc.co.uk/news/education-31733742 (Accessed September 2017).

Hattie, J. (2009) *Visible Learning*, London: Routledge.

Hoyle, A. (2017) 'What Happened When a Primary School Went Gender Neutral' at http://www.telegraph.co.uk/women/life/happened-primary-school-went-gender-neutral/.

Independent Teacher Workload Review Group (2016) *Eliminating Unnecessary Workload around Marking*. Crown Copyright. Available at: https://www.gov.uk/government/uploads/system/uploads/attachment_data/file/511256/Eliminating-unnecessary-workload-around-marking.pdf (Accessed September 2017).

Kohn, A. (2006) 'The Trouble with Rubrics', *English Journal*, 95:4, pp. 12–15.

Leonard, A. (2014) 'School Linking: Southern Perspectives on the South/North Educational Linking process: From Ghana, Uganda and Tanzania' Available at British Library: http://ethos.bl.uk/OrderDetails.do?uin=uk.bl.ethos.643018 and UCL Institute of Education http://eprints.ioe.ac.uk/21648/ (Accessed September 2017).

NECTA – National Examinations Council of Tanzania. Available at: http://www.necta.go.tz (Accessed November 2017).

Nelson, R., Spence-Thomas, K., and Taylor, C. (2015) *What Makes Great Pedagogy and Great Professional Development: Final Report Teaching Schools R&D Network National Themes Project 2012–14 Research Report Spring 2015*. Crown Copyright. Reference: DFE- RR443C Available at: www.gov.uk/government/publications (Accessed February 2018).

Quist-Adade, C., and van Wyk, A. (2007) 'The Role of NGOs in Canada and the USA in the Transformation of the Socio Cultural Structures in Africa,

Africa Development', *Council for the Development of Social Science Research in Africa*, 32:2, pp. 66–96.

Tan, A. L., and Towndrow, P. A. (2006) 'Giving Students a Voice in Science Practical Assessments', Paper presented at 32nd International Association for Educational Assessment Conference. Singapore.

Tirraoro, T. (2016) 'Head Teachers: Children with SEND Are Being Failed by Budget Cuts'. Available at: https://www.specialneedsjungle.com/head-teachers-warn-children-send-being-failed-budget-cuts (Accessed September 2017).

14

How can visually impaired children be supported?

One teacher's reflections on the bridge to cross on visual impairment in Tanzania

Baraka Mwiyoha and Alison Leonard

Visual impairments are a global issue, resulting in low or complete loss of vision, and there tend to be a high incidence in African countries. According to the World Health Organization (WHO, 2017), many sight problems are preventable, yet there is a persistent link between poverty and poor eye health. For children growing up in Tanzania, as in many sub-Saharan countries, visual impairment creates enormous challenges. Learning environments may be unfavourable to Visually Impaired (VI) students who often lack trained VI teachers and equipment (HakiElimu[1], 2008; Opini and Onditi, 2016). Additionally, traditional Tanzanian cultural beliefs have been an enduring hindrance to equality in education for VI pupils. The belief that

---

1   This Tanzanian NGO (Non-Government Organization) promotes inclusion of people with disabilities.

a child born blind or with Albinism is the result of a family curse has meant that many parents have been afraid to expose their VI children. Until recent times, their children had no value or rights; they were isolated, denied education, treatment, care or, in some cases, love. Although Tanzanian society has now become more knowledgeable about the causes and effects of visual impairment, there continue to be children who are unable to access formal education (Tungaraza, 2015).

How do cultural beliefs about 'impairments' in other countries affect access to education?

In recent decades, the Tanzania government has frequently reviewed its curriculum with the aims of improving inclusive education and Primary provision (URT, 2010). Tanzania's Special Education Needs (SEN) programme started in 1986 with three primary schools for the blind and a further nineteen units in primary schools (UNESCO, 1988). Since then, efforts have been made to improve quality, mode of delivery, curriculum content and teacher training for inclusive education. The government has been keen that school infrastructures offer inclusive learning environments for VI students and students with normal vision. Despite adjustments to the curriculum for secondary schools, some changes have not brought the expected or intended results. For instance, secondary students were previously excluded from science, basic mathematics, chemistry and physics, but from 2016 teachers had to find ways to implement practical methods and assessments for these subjects. Teachers' considerable endeavours to make them suitable for VI students did not bring about results that were equal to their sighted peers. Although VI students' apparent underperformance in national examinations may be due to the inadequacy of their examiners' expertise in Braille, it also meant that some students lost preparation and consolidation time. This would previously have enabled them to create Braille notes for lessons in other subjects. So while they experienced a broader range of subjects, many students struggled to develop depth of knowledge.

How can teachers and policymakers work harmoniously so that 'standards' are achievable and appropriate?

A challenge faced by teachers in many countries is meeting predetermined education goals. HakiElimu (2008) found that Tanzanian teachers had a difficult time designing and resourcing lessons. For teachers of VI students, the availability of Braille resources did not always match demand and there were insufficient teaching aids and reading materials. Sometimes materials were unreliable or no longer aligned to the Tanzanian syllabuses. Some teachers were ill equipped, or disinclined, to explore individual learning needs, or omitted to plan for a student's personal needs. Even when the stipulated curriculum content has been tailored to specific needs, successful outcomes may be unachievable for significant numbers of VI young people if teachers lack confidence or appropriate pedagogical knowledge (Tungaraza, 2015).

There are insufficient numbers of trained specialist VI teachers in Tanzania (Opini and Onditi, 2016) and many physical classrooms, including laboratories, are unsuitable for VI students. If a VI student's interactions with the learning materials are limited, comprehension and therefore progress may be slow. For instance, students regularly have to retain new information for several hours at a time, throughout six to nine lessons a day, before recording what they have covered in lessons at the start of the day. In such situations it is difficult to remember, complete follow-up exercises or thorough revision. Moreover, VI newcomers to a secondary school have to get used to and gain confidence in the layout of dormitories, classrooms, playgrounds, and so on. These students need time to become familiar with their new environment, and to form social relationships that will help them to adapt. If this is not factored in, VI students may develop a sense of being unwelcome or excluded and become demotivated. They need supportive companions, good mentors, teachers or guardians to encourage them to overcome their fears and uncertainties, to be high achievers in a world they cannot see.

Are truly inclusive learning environments a feasible reality?

Improving VI learning environments and resources in Tanzania seems possible if the intentions of education policies are fully implemented (URT, 2010). According to Opini and Onditi, policy measures are aimed at improving 'the educational status of children with disabilities by (i) developing disability policies, (ii) establishing inclusive schools, (iii) addressing the disability stigma, and (iv) improving teacher training' (2016, p. 67). Teacher training is listed as the final aim and is crucial. Making SEN training compulsory for all Tanzania's teachers would enable them to be better prepared for teaching in inclusive classrooms (Kiomoka, 2014). Professional trainers and teachers could be given regular Continuing Professional Development (CPD) and specific preparation time, in a similar manner to practitioners in other fields, to improve their knowledge and competences. Ideally, this would also enable them to develop their ability to improvize with materials at a time when there is a lack of commercial materials. There are already simple assistive technologies that provide practical solutions for inclusive education. These could make VI education more enjoyable and help prepare students with a range of essential skills (Leonard, 2018). However, as many technologies comprise of specialized, sophisticated packages that tend to be expensive, it is likely that adapting and designing basic tools will continue to be among the essential skills for Tanzanian teachers in the near future. Indeed, simple low- or medium-cost teaching resources, such as models, can be made from wood, and locally obtained soil, flora and rocks that are familiar to the students can provide good starting points for VI geographers. Field trips to nearby sites where students can learn by touching, smelling and feeling real-world environments are practical and affordable, but can also excite new exploration and understanding. While high-cost computers with scanning and reading software or 3D printers may not be readily available (DfID, 2010), feeling real objects can have significant impact on VI students' learning.

Furthermore, Tanzanian teachers who visited UK schools observed a distinct difference in staffing levels to those in their home schools, in particular, the provision of classroom teaching assistants. If similar support staff were deployed in Tanzania, they could bring enormous benefits for students and teachers in VI schools.

What practices are transferable between schools in different parts of the world?

The essence of inclusive education is that no student should be discriminated against or isolated. Though the safety, comfort and participation of all learners are undoubtedly important, it is also important to recognize that each VI student will have their own talents to be nurtured. All learners should have opportunities to improve their skills and lead fulfilling lives within, outside and beyond school. Yet, children with disabilities who are born into poverty in Tanzania are the least likely to go to school (Opini and Onditi, 2016). Sending their VI children to school is an enormous challenge for many families: schools need money for accommodating VI students' personal needs and when costs include learning materials or classroom support, this is often money they do not have. Children from poor families are often reliant on 'good Samaritans', businessmen, communities, government agencies and charitable organizations. Without financial support, VI students can become marginalized and lack chances to make progress in education. Providers should be enabling children to have equal access to good-quality education but it is often the case that ascertaining information about children with disabilities can be difficult. Having knowledge of each child's family background, their history and specific needs and their abilities can be crucial information for teachers (HakiElimu, 2018). Assessing the level of a VI student's understanding and learning difficulties can help in directing them to vocational training or an academic pathway, either of which can lead to worthwhile careers. Building on VI learners' talents and abilities could reduce the apparent boredom of students who may otherwise be stigmatized as 'slow learners' in Tanzanian classrooms that are not conducive to inclusion.

Every society needs to value people with special needs: 'Tanzania has moved from denial to inclusion, but inclusive education still faces daunting challenges' (Tungaraza, 2015, p. 111). Tanzanian society needs to wake up to the positive contributions that people with VI can bring, and to change societal perspectives of VI. Inclusion should be evident in every community, maybe starting with schools, but not just in schools.

How might such societal awareness be brought about?

Further reading

DfID (2010) 'Education for Children with Disabilities – Improving Access and Wuality. Guidance Note: A DfID Practice Paper'. Available at: https://www.gov.uk/government/uploads/system/uploads/attachment_data/file/67664/edu-chi-disabil-guid-note.pdf (Accessed April 2018).

HakiElimu (2008) *Do Children with Disability Have Equal Access to Education? A Research Report on Accessibility to Education for Children with Disabilities in Tanzanian Schools*, HakiElimu: Dar es Salaam, Tanzania.

HakiElimu (2018) *Examination of Learning and Participation of Visually Impaired Students in Inclusive Schools*. HakiElim: Dar es Salaam, Tanzania. Available at: http://www.hakielimu.org/files/publications/Research%20Report%20on%20inclusive%20education.pdf (Accessed April 2018).

Kiomaka, D. (2014) 'An Investigation of the Challenges Which Children with Visual Impairments Face in Learning and Participation in Inclusive Primary Schools'. Available at: https://brage.bibsys.no/xmlui/bitstream/handle/11250/278165/Kiomoka.pdf?sequence=1 (Accessed April 2018).

Leonard, A. (2018) 'The Role of Assistive Technologies in the Learning of Visually Impaired Young People at a Rural Tanzanian Secondary

School', in Xudong Zhu, Jiayong Li, Mang Li, Qiang Liu, Hugh Starkey (eds), *Proceedings of the 6th BNU / UCL IOE International Conference in Education*. Springer Press with Beijing Normal University (BNU) (Forthcoming publication).

Opini, B., and Onditi, H. (2016) 'Education for All and Students with Disability in Tanzanian Primary Schools: Challenges and Successes', *International Journal of Education Studies*, 3:2, pp. 65–76.

Tungaraza, F. (2015) 'The Arduous March toward Inclusive Education in Tanzania: Head Teachers' and Teachers' Perspectives', *Africa Today*, 61:2, pp. 108–23.

UNESCO (1988) *Special Education in Tanzania, Project Findings and Recommendations*, United Nations Educational Scientific and Cultural Organization, Paris. Available at: http://unesdoc.unesco.org/images/0007/000784/078420eo.pdf (Accessed April 2018).

URT (2010) *National Strategy for Growth and Reduction of Poverty II (NSGRP II)*, Available at: https://www.imf.org/external/pubs/ft/scr /2011/cr1117.pdf (Accessed June 2015).

World Health Organization (WHO) (2017) Available at: http://www.who.int/blindness/world_sight_day/2017/en/ (Accessed March 2018).

15

How do theory and practice relate to each other in the social reality of the classroom?

Recognizing the challenges of aligning school placement resources in South African townships with beliefs about educational equalities

Vuyokazi Nomlomo and Melanie B. Luckay

This chapter reflects on the design of a teaching practice model at one higher education institution in post-apartheid South Africa, which is guided by principles of critical reflection and making connections between theory and practice. It highlights the shifts that have occurred in teacher education since 1994, as the country transitioned from apartheid education to a democratic system. It argues that an imbalance in teacher education knowledge, the university and school contexts, as well as societal challenges, have a negative influence on the design of a teaching practice model in South Africa.

Teacher education institutions in South Africa developed out of nineteenth-century mission schools, which drew pupils from a multitude of races, tribes and languages (Moloantoa, 2016). Through the Bantu Education Act of 1953, the ruling National Party imposed a discriminatory apartheid policy that perpetuated racial inequality (Gerard, 2011; Modisaotsile, 2012; Kanjee et al., 2010; Chisholm, 2004; Chisholm, 2009; Rakometsi, 2008). The minimum educational skills with which Africans or black learners were provided also had a negative impact on the teacher training system, especially for black schools (Gerard, 2011; Chisholm, 2009; Thobejane, 2013; Rakometsi, 2008; Hartshorne, 1995).

The apartheid government used colleges of education to advance its discriminatory policies and to prevent African pupils' access to quality education. By 1961, while 96 per cent of teachers in white schools were qualified only 57 per cent of teachers in black schools were (HSRC Report, 2012). In fact, until the 1990s, there were 105 racially segregated colleges in South Africa training primary school teachers (Green et al., 2014; Kwenda and Robinson, 2010), with approximately two thirds of the colleges catering for black students in the Bantustans, or rural areas (HSRC Report, 2012). These were poorly resourced, had inadequately qualified teaching staff and resulted in low-level qualifications for primary teachers (Gerard, 2011).

Under the Bantustan system, teacher training programmes produced ill-prepared teachers, exacerbating the poor quality and low standards of primary education in black schools throughout the apartheid education system (Gerard, 2011; Muthivhi and Broom, 2008). This was not the case for white schools. There were wide variations in the teaching models that underpinned the design and structure of programmes and the culture of teaching (Green et al., 2014; Gerard, 2011). It is widely documented that the education of black children emphasized transmission teaching and rote learning (Muthivhi and Broom, 2008; Gerard, 2011; Hartshorne, 1995).

Why might such methods be regarded as stifling critical thinking and demanding submissive attention to the teacher?

The transformation in South African education began in 1994, and part of the agenda was to rationalize teacher education colleges (Gerard, 2011; Chisholm, 2009). A new qualifications framework and revised curriculum requirements were introduced, underpinned by principles of equity and social justice (Kwenda and Robinson, 2010). Teacher training colleges were relocated to universities in 2001, and a four-year Bachelor's Degree in Education (B.Ed.) replaced teacher training offered by colleges of education (Kwenda and Robinson, 2010; Chisholm, 2009). Nevertheless, the quality of teachers emerging from these institutions has continued to be a matter of concern in post-apartheid South African education (Kanjee et al., 2010).

How can re-positioning education policy affect social change?

Shifting teacher education to higher education forced universities to engage with teacher training in ways that had previously not been necessary (Samuel, 2002). Universities elevate theoretical knowledge (Robinson, 2015), but tend to downplay practical and pedagogical knowledge in school-based teaching practice. This is commonly referred to as the theory-practice divide (Gravett, 2012; Gravett and Ramasaroop, 2015). Moreover, South African policy documents have specified exit-level outcomes and competences to be assessed during teaching practice (Department of Education (DoE), 2000a; DoE 2015b), but not paid attention to how teacher educators should operationalize pedagogical knowledge during the teaching practice component to accomplish the outcomes.

How might the imperative to operationalize theoretical and practical knowledge in schools impact on teacher education?

Alongside the societal challenges in South Africa, an unbalanced model is likely to affect students' performance and perceptions of the profession (DoE, 2015b). In light of the above, we reflect on the teaching practice model at the University of the Western Cape (UWC), which is influenced by socio-economic factors such as societal inequality, unequal access to resources and school contexts. The model of teaching practice at UWC seeks to assess if and how theoretical orientations have been adopted in actual classroom practice with a strong focus on promoting self-conscious reflection (Robinson, 1999). In general, social constructionist and transformative approaches centring on emancipation, democracy, social justice and transformation shape university lectures. The aim is to develop teachers who are active, informed, critically reflective and prepared to change society (Robinson, 1999). Furthermore, practical and pedagogical orientations are steered by the cognitive apprenticeship model (Collins et al., 1987; Ndileleni et al., 2016) as proposed in Bandura's (1977) social learning theory. Yet the social realities suggest that many schools lack mentoring capacity, conceptual and pedagogical knowledge, physical resources and teachers have to cope with challenging learner behaviour (DoE, 2015b; Robinson, 2015, Van Wyk et al.,

2016). Such factors detract from the student teacher's ability to reflect as expected from the university's teaching practice model. As a consequence, it is argued that student teachers do not develop deep levels of reflection (Robinson, 1999), often struggling to reach the first level of reflection by the end of the programme. Thus, the impact of these challenges can counter the outcomes that the model of teaching practice is designed to accomplish.

To what extent can university content shape teaching practice?

The model of teaching practice at UWC is highly influenced by factors related to how the teaching practice is operationalized. The most important of these are the following factors: (1) time spent on teaching practice, (2) relationships with and at schools, (3) school readiness and resources. First, over the four-year period, the students spend a total of thirteen weeks on teaching practice. The length ranges from a period of one to two weeks to a seven-week period in the final year of the B.Ed. programme. Possibly a longer time of classroom-based teaching practice would allow for more meaningful and robust reflection as students tend to take time to become acculturated to a school's practices. Quick and Sieborger (2005) showed that both teachers and students support a longer time on teaching practice.

How much time is enough for students to reflect meaningfully?

Secondly, in the relationship between the schools and the university, it is expected that school mentors will support the university's teaching practice model. While the university should communicate the practice goals to schools, mentor teachers also need to indicate their requirements for the university to support the realities of the school context (Silbert and Verbreek, 2016). It seems there is a gap between the partnership and the university, which requires both the training of mentor teachers (Robinson, 2015) and greater exchange of information.

Should school and university partnerships be generic or context-specific?

Thirdly, the availability of resources should not define which schools are suitable for teacher education placements. The reflective teaching practice model can be effective in a range of school placements, even though the reality at UWC is that the majority of students are placed in poor or dysfunctional schools. This means teachers face heavy workloads and, in many instances, a lack of adequate physical infrastructure (Robinson, 1999, 2015). Furthermore, the university and students face high travel and accommodation costs, all of which result in the dilemma of choosing placement schools based on their readiness to support student teachers or convenience.

In conclusion, despite the efforts to transform teacher education in post-apartheid South Africa, the university and school contexts and the societal challenges each influence the design of the teaching practice model at the university. More research-based evidence is needed to interrogate the impact of such factors on teacher education programmes and students' ability to reflect on their experiences.

Further reading

Bandura, A. (1977) *Social Learning Theory*, Engelwood Cliffs, NJ: Prentice-Hall.

Chisholm, L. (2004) 'The Quality of Primary Education in South Africa', *The Quality Imperative*, Paper commissioned for the EFA Global Monitoring Report 2005.

Chisholm, L. (2009) 'The Debate about Re-opening Teacher Education Colleges', in *An Overview of Research, Policy and Practice in Teacher Supply and Demand 1994–2008*, Cape Town: Human Sciences Research Council, pp. 14–20.

Collins, A., Brown, J. S., and Newman, S. E. (1987) *Cognitive Apprenticeship: Teaching the Craft of Reading, Writing and Mathematics (Technical Report No. 403)*, Cambridge: BBN Laboratories.

Department of Education (DoE) (2000a) 'Norms and Standards for Educators', *Government Gazette*, 415:20844, 4 February 2000, Pretoria: Government Printers.

Department of Education (DoE) (2015b) *Minimum Requirement for Teacher for Teacher Education Qualification* (MRTEQ), South Africa: Department of Higher Education.

Gerard, A. (2011) *Apartheid Transition: Assessing a Black Township*, Rhode Island College: Digital Island Press.

Gravett, S. (2012) 'Crossing the 'Theory-Practice' Divide: Learning to Be(come) a Teacher', *South African Journal of Childhood Education*, 2:2, pp. 1–14.

Gravett, S., and Ramasaroop, S. (2015) 'Bridging the Theory and Practice in Teacher Education: Teaching Schools – a Bridge Too Far?', *Perspectives in Education*, 33:1, pp. 131–46.

Green, W., Adendorff, M., and Mathebula, B. (2014) 'Minding the Gap? A National Foundation Phase Teacher Supply and Demand Analysis: 2012–2020', *South African Journal of Childhood Education*, 4:2, pp. 1–23.

Hartshone, K. (1995) 'Language Policy in African Education: A Background to the Future', in Mesthrie, R. (ed.), *Studies in South African Sociolinguistics*, Cape Town: David Phillip, pp. 306–18.

Human Sciences Research Council (HSRC) Press (2012) *The Low Achievement Trap: Comparing Schooling in Botswana and South Africa*, Available at: www. hsrcpress. ac. za/downloadpdf. php?pdffile (Accessed May 2016).

Kanjee, A., Sayad, Y., and Rodriguez, D. (2010) 'Curriculum Planning and Reform in Sub-Saharan Africa', *Southern African Review of Education*, 16:1, pp. 83–96.

Kwend, C., and Robinson, M. (2010) 'Initial Teacher Education in Selected Southern and Eastern African Countries: Common Issues and Ongoing Challenges', *Southern African Review of Education*, 16:1, pp. 97–112.

Lewin, K., Samuel, M., and Sayed, Y. (eds) *Changing Patterns of Teacher Education in South Africa: Policy, Prospects and Practice*, Sandown: Heinemann.

Modisaotsile, B. (2012) *The Failing Standard of Basic Education in South Africa*. African Institute of South Africa (AISA), Policy Brief 72.

Moloantoa, D. (2016) *The Contested but Pivotal Legacy of Missionary Education in South Africa*. Available at: www. theheritageportal. co. za/article/ contested-pivotallegagcy-missionary-education (Accessed January 2018).

Muthivhi, E., and Broom, Y. (2008) 'Continuities across Schooling Transition: A Case of Classroom Practices among Venda Teachers in South Africa', *Journal of Educational Studies*, 7:1, pp. 98–121.

Ndileleni, M., Joubert, I., and Phatudi, N. (2016) 'Teaching Practice – Its Purpose and Implementation', in Okeke, C., Abonggdia, J., Olusola Adu, E., Van Wyk, M., and Woluter, C. (eds), *Learn to Teach: A Handbook for Teaching Practice*, South Africa: Oxford University Press.

Quick, G., and Sieborger, R. (2005) 'What Matters in Teaching Practice? The Perceptions of Schools and Students' *South African Journal of Education*, 25, pp. 1–4.

Rakometsi, M. (2008) 'The Transformation of Black Education in South Africa, 1950–1994: A Historical Perspective', (PhD thesis) Bloemfontein: University of the Free State.

Robinson, M. (1999) 'Initial Teacher Education in a Changing South Africa: Experiences, Reflections and Challenges', *Journal of Education for Teaching*, 29:1, pp. 191–201.

Robinson, M. (2015) *Teaching and Learning Together: The Establishment of Professional Practice Schools in South Africa* (report), Department of Higher Education, South Africa.

Samuel, M. (2002) 'Autobiographical Research in Teacher Education', in Lewin, K., Samuel, M., and Sayed, Y. (eds), *Changing Patterns of Teacher Education in South Africa: Policy, Prospects and Practice*, Sandown: Heinemann.

Silbert, P., and Verbreek, C. (2016) 'Partnerships in Action: Establishing a Model of Collaborative Support to Student and Mentor Teachers through University-School Partnership', *Journal of Education*, 64, pp. 111–36.

Thobejane, T. (2013) 'History of Apartheid Education and the Problems of Reconstruction in South Africa', *Sociology Study*, 3:1, pp. 1–12.

Van Wyk, M., Galloway, G., and Okeke, C. (2016) 'Basic Classroom Management', in Okeke, C., Abonggdia, J., Olusola Adu, E., Van Wyk, M., and Woluter, C. (eds), *Learn to Teach: A Handbook for Teaching Practice*, South Africa: Oxford University Press, pp. 236–50.

Part II

A view from the outside looking in

When you step outside your own education system and observe or partake in another country's education system it will raise various issues. There will be the familiar, maybe strange practices, certainly unfamiliar environments and almost certainly different cultures and philosophies. The chapters in Part II are a collection of writing by people who have experienced an aspect of education in a country other than their own.

16

What can we learn from two contrasting cultural educational traditions?

The reflections of an English lecturer prompted by working in Malaysia

Vanessa Young

This chapter will explore the implications of two very different approaches to education – Socratic and Confucian. It has been argued that 'Eastern' and 'Western' education systems are underpinned by these two traditions. I will draw on the work of Tweed and Lehman (2002) and consider experience in both Malaysian and English contexts. How does a 'Confucian' view contrast with a 'Socratic' one? What lessons can we, in 'The West', learn from a Confucian approach? Thinking about the work of Carol Dweck for example (2007, 2015), should we be placing more value on the Confucian notion of 'effortful learning' as opposed to ability and success? The chapter is based on my reflections as an education lecturer working as a consultant in Malaysia.

It was with excitement, and no small measure of trepidation, that we, as a team of tutors, flew from the UK to Malaysia for the start of a project that would prove to be a seminal experience for many of us. Our role: to support and facilitate the design and development of a new undergraduate degree with qualified teacher status for primary teachers in Malaysia. It was a real baptism of fire for most of us, as, although we had a common purpose, and the tutors we were collaborating with were also teacher educators, the culture in which we found ourselves was in some ways quite unfamiliar.

Over the course of the project (involving regular visits over four years), a specific range of challenges and questions gradually unfolded. The emergence of these was as much to do with our growing understanding of the culture, and the deepening of our relationships across the cultural bridge as with anything else. We became aware of some key differences between our 'home students' and the Malaysian students, not just in terms of culture, but also in approaches and attitudes to learning. These were reflected in the views of the Malaysian tutors and indeed the Ministry of Education.

The questions presented themselves in the form of dichotomies, three of which will be discussed in turn in due course. But first, the problematic nature of 'East' and 'West' terminology needs to be addressed. One cannot think geographically in this context, as Western conceptions of approaches to learning include countries from Australasia for instance. Rather, we have to think culturally about the traditions that underpin our education systems. There may also be huge differences between approaches to learning across the range of cultures and countries categorized within the terms 'East' and 'West', so I am aware of the dangers of oversimplification in using purely binary terms about East/West, Socratic/Confucian, particularly with respect to the interplay between them and the merging of cultures as a result of globalization. I proceed with these caveats in mind.

Effort versus ability

We first became aware that high value was placed on effort rather than just ability. It seemed Malaysian tutors were keen to give much more credit to the work and time the students had put into their work than our UK degree criteria would allow. Students working in the 'Western tradition' may achieve the same outcomes regardless of effort and the comment: 'Well tried!' is not always seen as complimentary. The Malaysian tutors genuinely admired and gave credit to the hard work of their students, and it was evident that the students themselves believed they could achieve if only they worked hard enough. Within the Confucian–Socratic framework (Tweed and Lehman, 2002), the idea that effort is central to the learning process is entirely consistent with Confucian values. The Malaysian approach exemplified an 'incremental' theory of intelligence, which views intelligence and ability as malleable traits which can be improved upon through effort and hard work (Dweck, 2007). It seemed that, surprisingly, we as UK tutors held much more of an 'entity' theory of intelligence, seeing ability as a fixed trait. According to this theory, if students perceive that their ability to perform a task is high, then they believe that they will have a good chance of mastering the task. Conversely, if they perceive their ability to be low, a feeling of hopelessness can hinder any possibility of mastery. This has been described as 'learned helplessness' (Hiroto and Seligman, 1975). This was a salutary realization as, back home, we as tutors would routinely proselytize Dweck's notion of 'growth mindset' to our own Initial Teacher Education (ITE) students, both in their approaches to their own learning and in their work with children. I wonder however if our conceptions of 'effort' in the west are somewhat limited. Dweck herself has more recently realized that this aspect of her Mindset Theory has been misunderstood in seeming to suggest that all students need to do is 'try' and they will achieve. She has countered this assumption with the term 'effortful learning'. This notion of 'trying' is significantly more nuanced. Here, students need to try new strategies and seek input from others when they are stuck. They need this repertoire of approaches – not just sheer effort – to learn and improve (Dweck, 2015). This made us question how we could encourage 'effortful learning' in our home students to counter any sense of learned helplessness.

To what extent do you think work should be judged purely on ability? What would effortful learning look like in your context?

Collaborative versus individual

Effortful learning involves seeking input from others. We noticed an attitude of 'all for one and one for all' with the Malaysian students. They relished opportunities to work collaboratively, were highly supportive of one another and achieved a good deal through this collective approach. Interestingly, in our collective planning of the content of the degree, notions of 'the self' were resisted. The Malaysian tutors seemed uncomfortable with the idea of 'self-esteem', 'self-concept' and 'self-reflection'. Concepts of 'self' we came to realize, were different within the 'Eastern' tradition. Here, the self is constructed and enacted in terms of human relatedness – interdependence and communality with others (Kanu, 2005). Encouraging students in the way of the 'Western' tradition to think about themselves as important entities in their own right, regardless of others, seemed to the Malaysians to be self-centred, self-indulgent and egotistical.

Related to this was the idea of 'independent learning' which we were trying, with limited success, to promote as part of the pedagogy of the new degree. This observation echoes the findings of Kanu (2005) in her research with Pakistani students. In her findings, one of her students declared: 'What is the purpose if I get everything and others get nothing ... I feel satisfied when we all succeed and we are all happy. I don't want disgrace for any of us attending the programme.' (Kanu, 2005, p. 502). In the Western tradition, the uniqueness and power of the individual is highly prized. Individuals are valued for their knowledge and their ability to use their knowledge to make their mark on the world (Hofstede, 2011). This is commensurate with a culture of competitiveness. In contrast, Eastern traditions value the potential of the individual to merge with the world. 'When a drop of water returns to the ocean, although it outwardly loses the identity of dropness, it gains the permanency of the everlasting ocean' (Shaffi, 1988, p. 37, in Sumsion, 1994). In contrast, it seemed that our home students were raised in a culture of self-absorption and divisiveness. How could we foster a more collaborative, supportive approach to learning in our own courses?

What opportunities do you get to learn collaboratively? What issues might you encounter when it comes to assessing collaborative learning?

Overt versus postponed questioning

A key feature of the Socratic approach to learning is that learning occurs through continuous questioning. Socrates believed that knowledge already resided within the student and that encouraging them to question would allow students to recognize and explore this knowledge for themselves and express personal hypotheses. With the Confucian approach, learning tends to be perceived as a four-stage process: (i) memorizing, (ii) understanding, (iii) applying and (iv) by questioning or modifying (Tweed and Lehman, 2002). Knowledge is seen as dynamic and non-dualistic (Sumsion, 1994). The practice of 'critiquing' then is postponed to the end of the learning process. In the Western tradition, on the other hand, the idea of students questioning and critiquing is deeply embedded in the culture of higher education and a key component of higher education assessment criteria. We found a reluctance in the Malaysian students to engage in the kind of question and answer exchanges – the dialogic approach – commonly adopted as a pedagogical strategy with our home students.

A further challenge for the students was asking them to question the work of those who were authorities within the field. Kanu in her work with teachers in South Asia observed something similar. 'The teachers resisted our "critical", "challenging", "questioning" and, no doubt, "emancipatory" approach to their learning and saw it as a combative approach that was not grounded in their lives and experiences because it violated some of their deepest beliefs about maintaining harmonious relations with others.' (Kanu, 2005, p. 506). The values of respect and deference are intrinsic to Malaysian culture and society. Furthermore, we can see in Kanu's observation how the Western approach jarred with another core Eastern value – collectivism. And all of this relates directly to Confucian approaches to learning which involve acquiring knowledge first, postponing that kind of questioning until adequate preparatory knowledge has been acquired. This acquisition of knowledge has sometimes been criticized as mere 'rote learning', but Confucius indicated that learners were not to 'parrot' the words of authorities, but truly to understand, and be reformed by, the knowledge therein (Tweed and Lehman, 2002, p. 92). This made us question the nature of so-called 'rote learning' and memorization. Were our students sometimes encouraged to ask naïve questions based on little knowledge? Is there not a place for memorization which later leads to understanding? As a musician, I thought about the kind of insight into a piece of music I gradually gain through the process of memorization and repeated practise.

What place does memorization and practice have in your learning context? What challenges do you encounter when you are asked to critique a work?

When one has been brought up within a particular culture, it is difficult to look beyond that culture.

> It is natural to continue to live in the world in which one was born, but to exclude the others from thought is to will to remain intellectually insular... Staying home all the time may serve one's comfort, but it does not serve curiosity, humanity, nor, in the long run, truth.
>
> (Scharfstein et al., 1978, p. 127, cited in Sumsion, 1994)

The early stages of the Malaysia project threw our own values and approaches into sharp relief, as if seeing them for the first time – the long-established idea of 'making the familiar unfamiliar' (Wagoner, 2008). In doing so, it forced us, as experienced tutors, to also make a journey of the mind – to look at our own practice through a new conceptual framework.

The two pathways of creativity are related and opposing processes: the former 'makes the unfamiliar familiar', whereas the latter 'makes the familiar unfamiliar' (Wagoner, 2008). We felt we had experienced both these processes through this project. There is, of course, a huge risk of oversimplification, 'It is only too easy to lift ideas out of their cultural contexts, to translate the terms in which they are expressed into familiar ones, and to come to plausible but misleading conclusions' (Scharfstein, 1978, p. 9, in Sumsion 1994). Similarly, it is necessary to guard against gross generalizations and uncritical enthusiasm for unfamiliar ideas (Sumsion, 1994). While it would not be healthy or feasible to simply transpose Eastern approaches into our own practice with 'home students', an openness to alternative perceptions and approaches can only enrich our understanding. This was a unique and humbling experience which bore rich fruit. As a team, the lessons we learned from the thinking and discussion arising from our work with the Malaysian students and tutors permeate our practice to this day.

What have you learned from engaging with others from a different culture?

Further reading

Altbach, P. (2015) 'Higher Education and the WTO: Globalization Run Amok', *International Higher Education*, 23:1, pp. 2–4.

Aronson, C., Fried, C., and Good, C. (2002) 'Reducing the Effects of Stereotype Threat on African American College Students by Shaping Theories of Intelligence', *Journal of Experimental Social Psychology*, 38:2, pp. 113–25.

Dweck, C. (2006) *Mindset*, New York: Random House.

Dweck, C. (2007) 'The Perils and Promises of Praise', *Educational Leadership*, 65:2, pp. 34–9.

Dweck, C. (2015) 'Carol Dweck Revisits the Growth Mindset', *Education Week*, 35:5, pp. 20–4.

Hiroto, D., and Seligman, M. (1975) 'Generality of Learned Helplessness in Man', *Journal of Personality and Social Psychology*, 31:2, p. 311.

Hofstede, G. (2011) 'Dimensionalizing Cultures: The Hofstede Model in Context', in *Online Readings in Psychology and Culture*, 2:1. Available at: https://doi.org/10.9707/2307-0919.1014 (Accessed February 2018).

Kanu, Y. (2005) 'Tensions and Dilemmas of Cross-Cultural Transfer of Knowledge: Post-Structural/Postcolonial Reflections on an Innovative

Teacher Education in Pakistan', *International Journal of Educational Development*, 25:5, pp. 493–513.

Martinko, M., and Gardner, W. (1982) 'Learned Helplessness: An Alternative Explanation for Performance Deficits', *Academy of Management Review*, 7:2, pp. 195–204.

Sumsion, J. (1994) 'An Exploration of Eastern Philosophy: Enhancing Understanding of Reflection', paper presented at the *Annual Conference of the Australian Association and a Key Component for Research in Education*, Newcastle: Institute of Early Childhood, Macquarie, November 1994.

Tweed, R., and Lehman, D. (2002) 'Learning Considered Within a Cultural Context, Confucian and Socratic Approaches', *American Psychologist*, 89, 57:2, pp. 89–99.

Wagoner, B. (2008) 'Making the Familiar Unfamiliar' (commentary), *Culture and Psychology*, 14:4, pp. 467–74.

Yeager, D., Johnson, R., Spitzer, B., Trzesniewski, K., Powers, J., and Dweck, C. (2014) 'The Far-Reaching Effects of Believing People Can Change: Implicit Theories of Personality Shape Stress, Health, and Achievement During Adolescence', *Journal of Personality and Social Psychology*, 106:6, p. 867.

17

How could this be?

The transformative power of a Norwegian teacher educator's visit to the UK

Hilde Tørnby

In November 2016, I travelled from Norway to Canterbury in the UK on an Erasmus visit together with three colleagues. Erasmus is a European community-funded exchange project enabling greater links between educational institutions. At the time, I did not think much more about it than it was another typical staff visit between colleges. How mistaken I was. The visit changed me; *it inspired me in ways beyond words*. I feel that this trip was a profound renewal of my dedication to teacher training.

In this paper, I will explore ideas of transformative experiences using my exchange visit as a reference point. I will look at what this change brought about in me, for my teaching and research. Much has been written about transformative experiences and learning (Mezirow, 2000; Paul 2014; Scoffham and Barnes, 2009; Østern, 2008, 2013). Despite their different approaches, they all have a fundamental similarity – that there is something that activates or ignites change. It may be an experience in a broader sense, such as an exchange visit, or one that occurs closer to home, such as encountering a piece of art.

What can bring about change? In your life, what has brought about change?

Paul (2014) describes how experiences can be transformative in a personal and epistemic way. While a personally transformative experience brings about profound change in a person's beliefs, preferences and ideas about self, an epistemically transformational experience gives new knowledge and insight that would not have been accessible without the experience. A slightly different model of transformative learning is offered by Scoffham and Barnes (2009, p. 268) in which there is no distinguishing between a personal or epistemic experience. Instead, they use 'powerful experience' which may entail both. In this model, an experience of importance sets off 'cognitive disturbance' which may lead to deep learning or denial. When a powerful experience leads to deep learning, it may arise in five dimensions: cognitive, social, emotional, existential and empowerment. Finally, such an experience will have a 'long-term impact on professional practice' (Scoffham and Barnes, 2009).

Østern (2008, 2013) addresses transformative experiences through an aesthetics lens. She suggests that responding aesthetically to something and then remaking an idea from one form into another (for example remediating a literary text into film or an experience into a painting,) an aesthetic transformation occurs (Østern, 2008). Furthermore, aesthetic learning processes change the learner in relation to self, human life, society or nature (Østern, 2013, p. 29–30).

How is this important in teaching contexts?

The visit to Canterbury Christ Church University consisted of distinct experiences much like pieces in a tapestry. First of all, we had the opportunity to partake in lectures ranging from primary education to master's level covering a variety of subjects. One lecture focused on children's inherent literacy and the fact that children do come from different backgrounds. Then, we attended a university conference about young refugees and the challenges they are facing. Finally, we visited an Academy school in an area of high deprivation where we observed teaching in different classes, as well as being given the opportunity to talk with staff members and administrators. All visitors felt and saw the staff's dedication to children's learning, growth and well-being. In essence, their wanting to better pupils' futures through education was clearly communicated.

Now, what was embedded in the happenings described above that brought about this change in me? Let me start with the final hours we were visiting the university. I believe this is when everything crystalized into metacognition. The final meeting consisted of the four members of staff from Oslo University College, members of staff from the host university, including a professor and the Dean of Education. All participants were asked to make a collage of the importance of the visit. In my picture a child emerged: a happy child holding flowers high, like balloons, everything sprinkled in glitter. The Child. I tried to formulate words in this meeting when we were to share our images, but since I felt this crystallization of the week so deeply, my eyes teared up. Not until later, on the plane home, did this immediate response materialize into thoughts and words.

> In all of this – the child's wellbeing and education was at the core. I feel that Canterbury Christ Church University has this extra devotion of wanting to make a difference in the world. A dedication rooted in the institution as well as in its staff. Recently I have found myself focusing more on the research-part of my work, than the idea of enabling future teachers to make a difference in their daily work. A long time ago, when I decided to become a teacher, this was my deep-felt motivation – to make a change – to see and help children tackling learning and life. So in essence, this motivation was renewed because I felt so strongly that Canterbury Christ University is founded upon this very idea.
>
> (From a letter dated December 2016 based on notes made on the plane home.)

By being challenged to respond aesthetically to our visit, new information arose. Impressions, observations and feelings from the days in Canterbury worked themselves into our collages. For me, recontextualizing our week aesthetically was a transformative experience (Østern 2008, 2013). In aesthetic work one uses the senses to learn and to express oneself. Consequently, this method, of making collages instead of a traditional final meeting, takes courage from the organizers as well as knowledge about aesthetic processes and transformation. While other people at this meeting did not cry, the task evoked responses that otherwise might not have surfaced. This may have been lost without the aesthetic approach.

What kind of aesthetic methods have you used in your studies or work?

The consequences of this visit may be subtle for the bystander. Yet, the impact of the exchange experience seeped into my teaching and communicating with the students. Studying texts of disadvantaged children like *Tracy Beaker*, connected well with the UK school visit. Addressing concerns about disadvantaged children in the Oslo area, and the fact that there is an increasing number of children living below the poverty line, became inevitable. Making students aware of the differences between Oslo schools became an important preparation for students' practice.

When visiting my students in school practice, I now notice more troubled children. In the eastern part of town, twelve- to thirteen-year-old students in an English class hardly know how to speak English and struggle to read from the PowerPoints *they* have prepared. On the other side of the city ten- to eleven-year-olds create beautiful picture books in their English class. The inequalities are a stark reminder of our mandate: to educate students for a better future.

Inspired by the Erasmus visit, my vision has been to fuel my students with the deep-felt love for the child I saw in a UK school. One of my students wisely said, 'Many children in the Oslo schools, do not have the possibility of being a child. They are care takers with adult concerns.'

How can teachers make a difference in school?

One major consequence in my teaching is a shift in focus – to educate students who will be child-centred, caring teachers. This personally transformative experience (Paul, 2014) brought about a major alteration in my professional perspective as well as a sincere dedication to making a difference in my students' lives. What is more, I have decided to dedicate my research to topics that can bring change to classrooms and teachers in the field. Using the terminology of Scoffham and Barnes (2009), the visit has established deep learning seen in the emotional and existential aspect of my working life (changed focus, changed understanding of role). Furthermore, it has empowered me to voice 'the child' in everything I teach and research.

On a final note, I wonder why this exchange had such a transformative effect on me and not necessarily the same influence on the colleagues who shared the experiences. The reasons may be numerous, hence, one will have to conduct more extensive research to find out. The event that stands out as crucial to my transformation was the aesthetic work, perhaps a 'readiness to change' (Scoffham and Barnes, 2009). Since I am a painter, this may have appealed to my inner resources for being open and ready for change is fundamental to any artistic work.

Further reading

Fullan, M., and Langworthy, M. (2014) A Rich Seam. How New Pedagogies Find Deep Learning, Pearson. Available at: http://www.michaelfullan.

ca/wpcontent/uploads/2014/01/3897.Rich_Seam_web.pdf (Accessed February 2017).

Kligyte, G. (2011) 'Transformation Narratives in Academic Practice', *International Journal for Academic Development*, 16:3, pp. 201–13.

Lysaker, J., and Furuness, S. (2011) 'Space for Transformation: Relational, Dialogic Pedagogy', *Journal of Transformative Education*, 9:3, pp. 183–7.

Mezirow, J. (2000) *Learning as Transformation: Critical Perspectives on a Theory in Progress*, San Francisco: Jossey Bass.

Østern, A.-L. (2008) 'Aktiv estetisk respons som utfordring i litteraturundervisning', in Hestnes, H., Ottesen, H., and Østern, A.-L. (eds), *Estetisk tilnærming til tekstarbeid i språkfagene*, Trondheim: Tapir akademisk forlag, pp. 15–23.

Østern, A.-L. (2013) 'Kunstneren som veileder for barns kunstmøte', in Østern, A.-L., Stavik-Karlsen, G., and Angelo, E. (eds), *Kunstpedagogikk og kunnskapsutvikling*, Oslo: Universitetsforlaget, pp. 19–36.

Østern, A.-L., Stavik-Karlsen, G., and Angelo, E. (2013) 'Vitensformer i estetisk praksis', in Østern, A.-L. Stavik-Karlsen, G., and Angelo E. (eds), *Kunstpedagogikk og kunnskapsutvikling*, Oslo: Universitetsforlaget, pp. 271–80.

Paul, L. (2014) *Transformative Experience*, Oxford: Oxford University Press.

Scoffham, S., and Barnes, J. (2009) 'Transformational Experiences and Deep Learning', *Journal of Education for Teaching*, 35:3, pp. 257–70.

Slavick, G., and Zimbardo, P. (2012) 'Transformational Teaching: The Theoretical Underpinnings, Basic Principles, and Core Methods', *Educational Psychology Review*, 24, pp. 569–608.

Wilson, J. (1991) *The Story of Tracy Beaker*, United Kingdom: Doubleday.

18

How can you build well-being in a culturally different context?

Supporting student teachers during an international placement in South Africa

Karen Collett

The need for teacher development programmes to offer student teachers a range of international teaching contexts is growing in stature in northern countries and to a lesser extent in the south (Olsen and Haggen, 2015a, Olsen, Bratland and Hagan, 2015b). Their main aim is to better prepare students as global teachers. Increasingly, European countries and, therefore, higher education institutions and schools find it necessary to address issues of multilingualism and cultural diversity, as they engage with the mass migration of asylum seekers and economic migrants from countries in Africa and the Middle East.

These changing school demographics have required teachers and teacher developers to shift attitudes, to review curriculum content and pedagogical practices, in order to respond to diverse learner needs. This has included giving greater attention to pastoral and psychological care, particularly for those learners and students who are survivors of war or trauma. Such factors have, in turn, raised the issue of teacher well-being and the best ways of addressing well-being in teacher development programmes (Collett and Olsen, 2012; Olsen et al., 2015a). When students have school placements, or practicums, in diverse contexts it can build their capacity to manage the challenges of a range of contexts. However, placing student teachers in multilingual and culturally diverse schools or in contexts prone to violence and trauma, can also increases their stress levels. Hence, the need to focus on integrating teacher well-being in teacher education and induction programmes, to assist teachers in understanding, coping with and taking agency to address the challenges they face (Collett et al., 2012).

What are the challenges of teaching a multilingual, culturally diverse class?

Drawing on the findings from a wider international placement programme for Norwegian students in South Africa, Olsen et al. (2015a, p. 161) found that an action research project focusing on teacher well-being provided 'an innovative approach to enhance their professional ability'. This chapter explores how the Teacher Well-Being (TWB) short course component, infused as part of the exchange model, influenced the professional development and resilience of the participating student teachers.

Olsen et al. (2015a, p. 158) found that the teacher well-being course helped students to prepare for some of the realities of the practice school and its community. The course was framed by philosophies of care and social justice (Tronto, 1993; 2013), beginning with the view that caring for the well-being of teachers strengthens their capacity to cope. Care is defined by Tronto (1993, p. 103) as 'everything that we do to maintain, continue and repair "our world" so that we can live in it as well as possible', a world that includes our environment, our bodies and ourselves (Tronto, 1993, p.103; Fisher and Tronto, 1990). Care is thus an activity and a disposition, which enables human flourishing through maintaining and repairing the world (Zembylas, Bozalek and Shefer, 2014). Zembylas et al. (2014) contend that Tronto's definition of care provides a useful framework to think about care as it is inclusive of self-care, it incorporates the environment and thus extends care beyond a human perspective. It views care as 'an ongoing social, political and emotional practice' (2014, p. 4). Each of the five phases of care was part of the TWB course: 'Caring about', 'Caring for', 'Caregiving', 'Care-receiving' and 'Caring-with' (Tronto, 1993, 2013). In the limited space of this Chapter I will focus on the aspect of 'Caring for'.

How is a culture of 'caring for' enacted in your educational institutions and courses? How might it permeate everyday ways of being?

'Caring for' is associated with the moral element of taking responsibility when a need is recognised. While this phase would address how a person is able to respond to and take responsibility for the needs of others, it is also a key principle of care in a social justice and democracy agenda (Zembylas et al., 2014). Responsibility is 'embedded in a set of implicit cultural practices rather than a set of formal rules' (Tronto 1993, cited in Zembylas et al., 2014, p. 5).

Responding to student needs within a short course requires shifting and adapting the content, pedagogy and design to prepare students for their international school placement. To meet students' personal and professional needs, the following definition of teacher well-being was used as a foundation for the course:

> A dynamic and holistic state of having, loving, meaning and being in one's personal and professional life, as a result of being part of a school community and this community's influence on the physical, social and cultural environment and working conditions in support of teaching and learning. (Collett, 2014, p. 137)

The course design was premised on an action learning and reflection model at a personal, interpersonal and collaborative level. Furthermore, the content and pedagogy encompassed a whole school development approach in which approaches to learning communities and organizational change were embedded (Dalin, 1998; Davidoff et al., 2014; Senge, 2002; Fullan, 2004; Wenger, 1998). Designing the TWB course flexibly over the duration of the practice placement ensured it was authentically responsive to new needs throughout. It began with a one-day orientation, continued with a day's workshop towards the middle and concluded with a day towards the end of the placement.

What knowledge and skills can equip student teachers to support their own and other's well-being?

Empowering student teachers to take agency to enable their own and other's well-being was a core focus in the course. This included sharing information on the factors supporting and constraining TWB in South African schools, as well as key theories and policy relating to school health promotion, System Theory (Bronfenbrenner, 1979) and whole school development. Another essential component was introducing the students to core life skills, such as stress management and mindfulness strategies (Collett, 2016, p. 1). Student feedback between 2014 and 2016 raised the need for increased awareness of their language barriers to learning and how these could impact their ability to cope in school or university. With Norwegian as their first language, many faced challenges in following spoken English and reading lengthy articles written in English. Through subsequent collaborative workshops and carefully paced sessions, the students were provided with ongoing opportunities that guided their understanding and experience in schools. In each of the sessions, an action-learning approach enabled new issues to be raised and strategies at a personal, professional and whole school level to be discussed. Building a strong action-learning element into the course helped to enhance student teacher agency, their capacity to respond to their own needs and to those of their peers and placement teachers. Individual and collaborative processes of reflection on action through a caring and collaborative community of practice enabled the identification of coping needs and appropriate responses. Olsen et al. argue 'that the opportunities provided for reflective practice together with the teachers ... seem to have enhanced the students' cultural insights, respect and understanding significantly' (2015a, p. 161).

What is your understanding of the opportunities for critical reflexivity afforded by teaching across cultures?

Additionally, teaching specific skills in solution-focused counselling helped students to provide interpersonal support for each other. These sessions offered them an extended range of skills they could draw upon if they were required to address the immediate needs of learners, peers or colleagues in their school. The flexible nature of the course allowed relevant content to be added to the curriculum as it progressed. This included exploring differences between inclusive education support in Norwegian and South African schools, strategies to address multilingual classes and teaching large classes.

While the frame of TWB within a whole school and systemic approach helped to focus responsibility for addressing well-being at a school and systems level, not only at an individual level, addressing these broader school issues was not possible for student teachers. However, raising awareness helped to sensitize them to contextual conditions influencing well-being and the potential for tackling these constraints through a whole school and broader developmental approach.

The research by Olsen et al. (2015a and 2015b) revealed that the TWB course on its own could not respond adequately to all student teachers' coping needs. Developing strategies to deal with the cultural complexities of corporal punishment or learner violence, for example, require specific sustained pre-service support, as well as ongoing developmental interventions in the placement schools themselves. Nonetheless, a focus on teacher well-being was found to provide students with the observation and reflexivity capabilities to collaboratively manage experiences that shocked them during their international placement. The course played a role in building conditions of trust and solidarity between the student teachers at an interpersonal level, although issues of trust and solidarity at a school level were more complex. Olsen et al. (2015b, p. 14) found that tensions between student teachers and school value systems, and practices in addressing and disciplining children, resulted in students expressing anger and frustration. This could negatively affect the respect and openness being built between people from different cultural backgrounds.

To what extent is it possible to be culturally responsive when faced with practices that are abhorrent in your own culture?

Although all schools in which student teachers were placed had been part of a TWB project intervention which sought to develop a caring and supportive school culture (Collett and Olsen, 2012), a caring culture was not always sustained. This raises the need to pay close attention to enhancing both the well-being needs of student teachers, as well as teachers and schools in the placement context. Attention to care for student teachers can be supported through a stronger teacher well-being focus in pre-service training programmes (Collett et al., 2012) and a TWB course in placement programmes. Moreover, good caring would require increased levels of support in practice placement schools to enhance a whole school development approach to nurture and sustain conditions for teacher well-being. This is particularly important in diverse multilingual and multicultural school contexts, and in contexts where violence and trauma are part of the day to day teaching experience. For higher education institutions it raises a challenging question about the sorts of partnerships that are necessary between international HEI's and local school partners to build an environment within which the well-being of student teachers can be supported and sustained.

Further reading

Bronfenbrenner, U. (1979). *The Ecology of Human Development: Experiments by Nature and Design*, Cambridge: Harvard University Press.

Collett, K., and Olsen, S. (2012) 'Teacher Well-Being – a Successful Approach to Promoting Quality Education? – a Case Study from South Africa', in *Conference Proceedings 4th Paris International Congress of Humanities and Social Sciences Research*, Paris, July 2012.

Collett, K. (2013) *Report on TWB Course*, Cape Town: Unpublished internal course report.

Collett, K. (2014) 'Teacher Perceptions of the Role of a Primary School Principal in Supporting Their Well-Being: Learning from a School in Challenging Conditions' (Unpublished PhD thesis), Bellville: University of the Western Cape.

Collett, K. (2014) *Reflective Meeting Notes: July 2014* (Unpublished document).

Collett, K. (2015) *Short Course Report* (Unpublished internal document).

Collett, K. (2016) *TWB Course Outline and Programme* (Unpublished course document).

Dalin, P. (1998) *School Development: Theories and Strategies*, London: Continuum.

Davidoff, S., Lazarus, S., and Moolla, N. (2014) *The Learning School: A Psycho-social Approach to School Development* (3rd edn), Cape Town: Juta.

Fisher, B., and Tronto, J. (1990) 'Towards a Feminist Theory of Caring', in Able E., and Nelson, M. (eds), *Circles of Care: Work and Identity in Women's Lives*, Albany: State University of New York Press, pp. 35–62.

Fullan, M. (2004) *Leading in a Culture of Change: Personal Action Guide and Workbook*, San Francisco: Jossey-Bass.

Olsen, S., and Hagen, A. (2015a) 'How Can Exposure to Practice in a Foreign Context Enhance the Professional Development of Teacher Students? Case Study from South Africa', *Journal of the European Teacher Education Network*, 10, pp. 154–64.

Olsen, S., Bratland, K., and Hagen, A. (2015b) 'Preparing Student Teachers and Teachers for the Multicultural School and Preschool through International Practicum and Collaboration', in *Proceedings of The 40th Annual Conference of the Association for Teacher Education in Europe* (ATEE), Glasgow.

Senge, P. (2000) *Schools That Learn*, New York: Doubleday Dell.

Tronto, J. (1993) *Moral Boundaries: A Political Argument for an Ethic of Care*, New York: Routledge.

Tronto, J. (2013) *Caring Democracy: Markets, Equality, and Justice*, New York: NYU Press.

Wenger, E. (1998) *Communities of Practice: Learning, Meaning, and Identity*, Cambridge: Cambridge University Press.

Zembylas, M., Bozalek, V., and Shefer, T. (2014) 'Tronto's Notion of *Privileged Irresponsibility* and the Reconceptualization of Care: Implications for Critical Pedagogies of Emotion in Higher Education', *Gender and Education*, 26:3, pp. 200–14.

19

How can international exchange programmes support teacher development?

Norwegian student teachers' insights into their international experiences

Sissel Tove Olsen and Anikke Hagen

This chapter describes and analyses the experiences of preschool and primary school student teachers at Oslo Metropolitan University (OsloMet) during their three-month period of residence in South Africa. The students follow a programme for practical school experience and field studies in this foreign context and the focus here is on the impact this may have for student learning. The programme has been established at OsloMet to provide scope for learning and reflection, and to apply theoretical aspects of teacher education. The academic assignments provide a platform to discuss the mutually reinforcing benefits of practical experience and academic learning.

During their South Africa residence, the students live with local host families with links to the school, usually a family of one of the teachers, with a view to providing an arena for shared reflection and learning, as well as first-hand insights into local culture and ways of life. The legacy of apartheid is still very visible in South Africa. This is clearly reflected in the difference between resource-rich and resource-poor schools. The schools discussed here belong to the latter category, with pupils from very poor urban and semi-urban areas (townships) in and around the towns of Cape Town and Paarl. The pupils are exclusively from 'black' and 'coloured' population groups. The schools' local communities are characterized by very high unemployment (up to 40%), widespread alcohol and drug abuse, HIV/AIDS, tuberculosis, domestic violence, sexual abuse and teenage pregnancies (Olsen, 2013).

The basis of this chapter is a qualitative research study, which demanded the interpretation of data rather than quantitative measuring. Data collecting was undertaken from 2012 to 2015 with the objective of capturing both the complexity and the nuances of the phenomenon being examined (Miles and Hubermann, 1994).

The thirty-four participants consisted of four groups of Norwegian primary and preschool student teachers. Focus groups interviews, using open-ended questions, enabled the elicitation of a range of views, attitudes, perceptions and motivations (Johannessen et al., 2011). Additionally, written questionnaires were used for individual anonymized responses. All of the participants had experience of practical teaching in Norwegian kindergartens and schools and therefore had first-hand knowledge of classrooms in their home country. Interviews were conducted both during the students' stay in South Africa and after they returned to Norway. In analysing the data, considerable importance was attached to the way the participants themselves interpreted and understood their experiences at the schools. On the whole, they spoke openly, freely and enthusiastically, expressing both similarities and differences with regard to their experiences at the school and from living with the host family.

What methods would you use to capture qualitative date?

A majority of the students said that the preliminary theoretical studies undertaken before departure from Norway were very helpful in understanding the challenges posed by teaching in South African schools. They, nevertheless, described their first impressions as overwhelming and to some extent shocking. They spent a long time processing what they had seen and heard in order to understand both the context and their own feelings and reactions. This relates, for example, to the high teacher/learner ratio, dominant teacher-centred teaching methods, teachers' common use of harsh language towards learners and experiencing learners severely affected by extreme poverty.

The Norwegian students each received a warm reception from staff when they arrived at schools. Their cooperating teachers expressed high expectations of students' knowledge and their active participation in teaching, showing confidence in them as equal partners. The students quickly took responsibility for classes and had opportunities to try out their own methods of class management and didactics. The students described the combination of being entrusted with substantial responsibility and given demanding tasks as frightening and challenging, but also as important factors in promoting personal growth, giving them security and confidence in their professional identity. The following statement can serve as an example of students' reactions to this experience: 'You learn far more when you step outside your comfort zone … when you push beyond your own boundaries, you learn a lot.'

According to Heggen and Raaen (2014), reflexive professional practice is dependent on conscious awareness of the fundamental values and discourses that form the foundation for a student's pre-service training. Studies on students' experiences during teaching practice and studies abroad also reveal the need to be conscious of personal and professional values or biases (Ochoa, 2012; Brennan and Cusher, 2007). Students are carriers of cultural codes (Ochoa, 2012) and they need to be clear about how these determine their views and responses if they are to be able to reflect on their experiences rather than just describe them.

What values and cultural codes do you bring to your own practice?

The students' reflections on their experiences in South Africa show, nonetheless, that it was not easy to apply knowledge and understanding acquired in Norway in the new arena. Our interpretation of the students' reflections reveal that this is in line with van Oers' findings (2014) that coherence cannot simply be achieved by transferring knowledge from one context to another. According to Heggen and Raaen (2014) a number of researchers support van Oers in his assertion that all learning must be reformed (reconceptualized and negotiated) for use in a new situation. Heggen and Raaen (2014) therefore conclude that coherence also includes 'helping students to reconceptualize knowledge they have developed in one learning arena to another' (2014, p. 9). Our findings show that a number of students reconceptualize their prior knowledge from Norway by using the structure provided for reflection. Christensen et al.'s (2014) study of student teachers' experience in two learning arenas, OsloMet and their practice school in Oslo, introduces a new concept to illustrate how they understand the transformation of knowledge from the theoretical to the practical part of teacher education. They conclude that students rather than *transferring* what have they learnt in a theoretical, research-based context need to *translate* it to fit the practical teaching situation.

To what extent do you reconceptualize and negotiate learning in your own practice? Give some examples.

Our study shows that a number of students found the living arrangements afforded important opportunities for rewarding discussions with the host family, helping them to achieve a deeper understanding of the local community. This enabled insights into the children's lives outside school which influence their behaviour in school and their opportunities for learning.

In what ways does home life intersect with school performance?

The opportunity for practical experience in South Africa, combining school experience with academic studies and a range of contexts for systematic reflection, had a significant impact on students' learning. This was affective on a professional as well as a personal level. There are indications that the students experienced an increased awareness of the knowledge and values they took with them from their teacher-training programme, developing deeper appreciation of the inter-relationship between theory and practice. They also moved in the direction of a stronger sensitivity to the local context. During the interviews, it emerged that many of the students had no previous experience of being the outsider, different from the norm. The experience of having characteristics attributed to them on the basis of their appearance and background was new to them. Dahl (2004) refers to this as attribution, that is, one party attributes an opinion, attitude or quality to another party (p. 31). He maintains that attribution is a common response to new situations: we interpret and try to make sense of them based on our own frame of reference. The students say that these experiences have increased their awareness of their own predispositions, of how they also ascribe motives to other people on the basis of their own perceptions of them, with a tendency to fall back on prejudices and stereotypes in their descriptions of 'the others'.

The students maintain that the experience of being 'the one who does not understand' is one of the most important insights they acquired. They say that this insight has strengthened their sensitivity to and empathy towards other people and believe that they will be more sensitive and empathetic towards minority children and their parents in Norwegian schools and kindergartens. Wenger (2008) emphasizes the importance of unpleasant experiences for learning and reflection: 'There are times in our lives when learning intensified; when situation shakes our sense of familiarity, when we are challenged beyond our ability to respond, when we wish to engage in new practices and seek to join new communities' (Wenger, 2008, p. 8).

In general, students' asserted that the knowledge and experience they gained from their stay in South Africa increased their confidence and competence in their future role as teachers in their home country. In particular, they maintained that this would benefit their future communication with minority language pupils as well as the pupils' parents/guardians in Norway. The students also emphasized the importance of having direct personal experience of belonging to a minority. They regarded the increased empathy that ensued as a very important factor in communication with pupils in the same situation.

Discuss the sustainability of the promising impact flowing from this placement programme. What measures could be put in place to enhance the sustainability?

Further reading

Christensen, H., Eritsland, A., and Havnes, A. (2014) 'Bridging the Gap? Student Attitudes about Two Learning Arenas in Teacher Education. A Study of Secondary Teacher Students' Experiences in University and Practice', in Arntzen, E. (ed.), *Educating for the Future: Proceedings of the ATEE 38th Annual Conference, Halden 2013. Curricula in Teacher Education.* ATEE – Association for Teacher Education in Europe, pp. 46–61.
Cushner, K., and Brennan, S. (2007) 'The Value of Learning to Teach in Another Culture', in Cushner, K., and Brennan, S. (eds), *Intercultural Student Teaching: A Bridge to Global Competence*, Maryland: Rowman & Littlefield Education, pp. 1–12.
Dahl, Øyvind (2004). *Meetings between People: Intercultural Communication*, Oslo: Gyldendal. 4th ed.
Heggen, K., and Raaen, F. (2014) 'Koherens i lærerutdanninga' [Coherence in Teacher Education], *Norsk Pedagogisk*, Tidsskrift, 1, pp. 1–13.

Johannessen, A., Tufte, P., and Christoffersen L. (2011) *Introduksjon til samfunnsvitenskapelig metode* [Introduction to Scientific Method], Oslo: Abstrakt forlag 4.utg.

Miles, M., and Huberman, M. (1994) *Qualitative Data Analysis: An Expanded Sourcebook* (2nd edn), Thousand Oaks: Sage.

Ochoa, A. (2012) 'International Education in Higher Education: A Developing Process of Engagement in Teacher Preparation Programs', in Quezada, R. (ed.), *Internationalization of Teacher Educators for the 21st Century*, Abingdon: Routledge, pp. 103–13.

Olsen, S. (2013) 'Support to Teachers in a Context of Educational Change and Poverty: A Case Study from South Africa', *Policy in Futures Education*, 11:3. Available at: www.wwwords.co.uk/PFIE.

Wenger, É. (2008) *Communities of Practice: Learning, Meaning, and Identity*, Cambridge: Cambridge University Press.

20

How might teachers adapt their practice in response to traumatized students?

UK teachers teaching Yazidi children in a Greek refugee camp

Jill Matthews

After several decades of classroom teaching and ten years as a lecturer in education, the art of teaching continues to fascinate and puzzle me. There are many people within and outside of the field of education who profess to have found the answers to successful teaching and learning. For example, Lemov (2015) claims that rigorously following the set of classroom management techniques he has identified is an essential way to motivate all students to achieve. Yet others suggest that the quality of interactions with learners, known as relational pedagogy, is at the heart of effective teaching (Noddings, 1998; Degotardi and Pearson, 2014). While using a combination of approaches may provide more answers than a simplistic binary stance, it does seem that teaching is a complex art requiring sensitive, nuanced exchanges with infinite variations of individual learners.

How do you understand the art of teaching? What actions have you found which lead to effective learning?

Being open to every opportunity for professional learning can also help teachers to become better at teaching, more aware of the learning needs of the children, of how to structure the content and recognize small steps of genuine progress. The value of these principles was particularly apparent in 2016 when I volunteered for teaching Yazidi refugee children in Northern Greece. The group of some three hundred Yazidi refugees had left their homeland in Northern Iraq following the genocide in May 2016. They came from different settlements and had not yet formed a cohesive community group. While some families had managed to keep together, others were parted from relatives. Some children had become separated from their parents and were being cared for by grandparents, aunts and uncles. Having moved through many camps, they were finally housed in a large school type building with several families to a room. There were bunk beds to sleep on or mattresses placed on the floor. There were families and groups of single men settled into temporary 'pods' or plastic lean-to structures. Portable toilets and showers were stationed on the periphery of the yard. There was no hot water, but there were external taps of non-drinking cold water and hosepipes available. At the far end of the campus, the charity Médecins Sans Frontières had erected two large tents from which mental health support and basic health care were offered.

On our arrival at the camp the representative of one of the charitable organizations running it greeted us. A few children were playing outside; they stopped playing, quietly observing the new volunteers. As I turned to speak to our host, a small stone hit my back, perhaps indicative of the children's feelings towards strangers (Trentacosta et al., 2016). They quickly ran away, disappearing from view.

What do you regard as essential resources for teaching a new group of children?

As one of a team of volunteer teachers, my role was to support the children between the ages of four and eleven with educational activities. The classroom consisted of a groundsheet spread under a small tree, which afforded a little shade. The teaching materials comprised a few pairs of scissors, some fine point felt-tip pens, A4 white paper, wool, alphabet flash cards, a set of picture dominoes and a ball. The first principle the teaching team worked to was establishing a sense of trust so that the children would feel confident enough to come into the classroom area and from there to participate in the lessons being offered.

However, establishing a rapport with adults in the camp actually provided the route to working with the children. Time spent with the men each day, allowing them to come and go, to learn a few new phrases in English and to colour with the felt pens was not only therapeutic for them, but gradually encouraged the children to show their curiosity and to venture into the classroom. There are aspects of this methodology that, though superficially appear intuitive, could be said to exemplify the Steiner Waldorf approach (Nicol, 2016), which advocates that children learn best through imitating others and by learning alongside peers and adults.

In what ways might this be relevant to teaching in your own schools?

One volunteer teacher had taken a set of face paints. She started to paint the face of another volunteer and gradually some of the girls moved closer to watch. Other volunteers played with the ball, initially throwing and catching, but when they began playing basketball the older children also joined in. Gradually the children started to relax so that after the first week, they were joining the volunteers on visits to a hypermarket specializing in educational materials. These were followed by a visit to a Chinese supermarket to buy wool, knitting needles and crotchet hooks to encourage the refugee women to engage in activities. The children began to arrive early at the classroom, anticipating new activities or familiar treats such as having their faces painted or participating in group games. How important gaining the trust of the whole community proved to be. By working with the adult men on a daily basis, the children were able to see a routine being established, incrementally gaining confidence to sit with us under the tree playing simple games such as noughts and crosses and Pelmanism, or singing nursery and counting rhymes, and learning words in English.

How much time do you spend as part of your school day giving children the chance to indulge in familiar confidence building or relaxation activities?

In the second week, the weather changed and it became cold and wet. A group of us embarked on mathematical activities in the mornings. We were able to use one of the Médecins Sans Frontières' tents. For the volunteer teachers, the language barrier and the lack of materials were tangible challenges, but the children's experiences presented different barriers. Though these are issues we had not have previously experienced, they may be familiar to many teachers working with traumatized students. We started by playing simple games with each other (Pelmanism, find the pair, dominoes, noughts and crosses) as we waited for all the children to arrive. The ratio of adult to child was initially two adults to one child. To begin with they just watched but gradually they joined in with the games. Each day, more came and joined us. Using fingers as manipulatives, we started counting, introducing new terms such as 'more than' and 'less than' with written symbols. Acting on our request, the children collected the tops of drinking water bottles and we used these as counters. We devised a game using a 100-number grid. Some children aged seven and over soon acquired the language to demonstrate their ability to count to 100 and above, either in ones or tens, and could spot missing numbers. With the older children, we introduced simple activities which would lead to investigations, such as square numbers, triangular numbers and leaping frogs.

About ten children came regularly and were able to spend up to an hour or so with us. Others would sit down for ten minutes, play one game and then go. Others came, sat down to play and then wrecked the game or started a fight. We felt it was important that they should have freedom to participate or not, but we were quite clear in reprimanding undesirable behaviour. We tried to make it evident that though the negative disruptive behaviour was unacceptable, the child was always welcome if they joined in constructively. Often we were able to distract them by offering some of the colouring sheets and felt pens, which enabled them to stay within the tent and watch from a distance. The other volunteers leading language activities took a similar approach.

How can you establish a positive learning ethos in your classroom? How much time is available for nurturing pro-social behaviours?

Over time, a small core of about thirty children started to regularly attend full morning sessions, with one hour devoted to mathematics activities and one hour to language development. Nearly sixty children were able to participate in the afternoon creative activity sessions (usually making something like a mask,) or organized games. After the older students had attended formal school lessons in the mornings, they provided additional support with the younger children in the afternoons. Nevertheless, there continued to be a significant number of children who hovered on the edges, not quite able to join in but who were beginning to show an interest.

This experience confirmed my belief that effective teaching and learning cannot occur until the learners feel relaxed and confident in their environment. The refugee children had experienced atrocities beyond the scope of my imagination: they had seen people shot, endured the dangers of travelling overland through hostile territories, crossing the Mediterranean in dinghies and had experienced the deprivations of living in various camps before settling in Filippiada. They needed to develop trust in us as adult strangers before any learning could occur. In our schools, there are some children who find it similarly difficult to adjust to the new environment and codes of acceptable behaviour. The key to engaging these children in their learning lay in enabling them to relax and in finding activities that engrossed them while discretely giving appropriate support. Through active engagement in such tasks, confidence, language and learning began to develop. Minimizing the pressure enabled the children time to succeed.

Further reading

Degotardi, S., and Pearson, E. (2014) *The Relationship Worlds of Infants and Toddlers: Multiple Perspectives from Early Years Theory and Practice*, Maidenhead: Open University Press.

Jabbar, S., and Betawi, A. (2018) 'Children Express: War and Peace Themes in the Drawings of Iraqi Refugee Children in Jordan', *International Journal of Adolescence and Youth*, pp. 1–18.

Lemov, D. (2015) *Teach Like a Champion 2.0: 62 Techniques That Put Students on the Path to College*, San Francisco: Jossey-Bass.

Médecins Sans Frontières. Available at: https://www.msf.org. uk/?gclid=EAIaIQobChMI-ST_MW32gIVzL3tCh3BrAlUEAAYASAAEgLe dvD_BwE (Accessed March 2018).

Nicol, J. (2016) *Bringing the Steiner Waldorf Approach to Your Early Years Practice*, London: Routledge.

Noddings, N. (1988) 'An Ethic of Caring and Its Implications for Instructional Arrangements', *American Journal of Education*, 96:2, pp. 215–30.

Relational Pedagogy in Nordic Countries. Available at: http:// relationellpedagogik.se/relational%20pedagogy.html (Accessed March 2018).

Sirin, S., and Rogers-Sirin, L. (2015) *The Educational and Mental Health Needs of Syrian Refugee Children*, Washington, DC: Migration Policy Institute.

Taylor, S., and Sidhu, R. (2012) 'Supporting Refugee Students in Schools: What Constitutes Inclusive Education?', *International Journal of Inclusive Education*, 16:1, pp. 39–56.

Trentacosta, C., McLear, C., Ziadni, M., Lumley, M., and Arfken, C. (2016) 'Potentially Traumatic Events and Mental Health Problems among Children of Iraqi Refugees: The Roles of Relationships with Parents and Feelings about School', *American Journal of Orthopsychiatry*, 86:4, p. 384.

21

What do children think about other nations, peoples and cultures?

International research into children's perceptions of other lives and the implications for teachers

Stephen Scoffham

We live in a world which is interconnected as never before – a world in which trade, travel and electronic communications link people in complex and unpredictable ways. Most of the food that we eat, for example, comes from plants which originated in other places even if it is not imported directly. Similarly, we buy large quantities of clothes and consumer goods that have been made abroad. At the same time, news events which have happened many thousands of miles away are beamed into our homes on a regular basis. Meanwhile, millions of people travel overseas each year for their holidays in search of different environments and experiences. It is hardly surprising that children become aware of other nations, peoples and cultures from an early age. However, quite how they develop their ideas is still rather poorly understood (Beneker et al., 2013).

One way to find out more about children's ideas about the wider world is simply to ask them to list the countries they can name. Studies conducted with school children aged between seven and eleven in different countries over a number of decades (Jahoda, 1962; Wiegand, 2006; Reynolds and Winterek, 2016) have yielded broadly similar results. Typically children aged seven name around half a dozen countries, while those aged eleven name between fifteen and thirty. Countries which are either physically close or which have historical or cultural ties tend to feature most prominently in children's lists. Conversely, countries which are far away in terms of distance or which are politically isolated appear almost completely unknown to many youngsters. Interestingly, despite a widespread perception that children know less about the world now than in the past, this is not confirmed by research. Indeed, a longitudinal study of Swedish children in 1968 and 2013 revealed little overall change (Hennerdal, 2016).

What countries can you list and how do you account for any patterns (and gaps) in your knowledge?

Another way to establish children's world knowledge is to ask them to draw a map from memory. This is quite a demanding task which involves drawing ability and spatial skills as well as place knowledge. The most basic representations tend to show isolated circles and shapes representing not only countries, but also towns, iconic buildings and imaginary places (Wiegand, 2006). More sophisticated maps portray territories which are differentiated in terms of size and shape. The most advanced maps approximate to conventional representations of the continents and oceans presented in atlases and on the internet. Lowes (2008) notes that in the interim stages children often portray land masses surrounded by sea (island maps) or land masses clinging to the frame (edge maps). It also appears that both children and adults have a tendency to produce maps that are symmetrical and neatly aligned.

The enormous growth of children's world knowledge between age eight and eleven is particularly notable. However, the sheer variability of children's knowledge is also striking. Researchers account for this in a number of ways. Parents, peers and education are seen as significant influences, as are travel experiences. Barrett (2007) draws attention to the way multiple social and cultural factors interact and argues from an extensive review of research that gender, social class, nationality, ethnicity and geographical location all contribute to children's global understanding. Being aware of these different factors is important if schools are to devise effective teaching programmes.

On the surface, teaching children about other nations appears to be relatively straight-forward and uncontentious. Yet, even the most basic facts are often open to interpretation. For example, some countries like the Ukraine, Morocco and India have disputed borders. Others such as Greenland are semi-independent. Tibet was once independent but is now increasingly recognized as part of China. Some groups of people such as the Kurds and Palestinians want to establish their own country but have not been able to do so. There is nothing abstract about these issues as they have a huge impact on people's lives. The way that countries are shown on the world map also makes a difference. By convention north is shown at the top of the map which positions Europe above Africa and North America above South America implying their superiority. If this seems a fanciful claim try turning the world map 'upside down' by putting south at the top. It is quite a disturbing experience!

Children express preferences for different countries from an early age. Unsurprisingly, pupils generally express a liking for their own country and to prioritise its interests over that of others (Beneker et al., 2013). They also tend to see their own way of life as being right. There is evidence that some children may develop negative attitudes to countries they perceive as being different to their own (Stilwell and Spencer, 1973). Several studies note that children express a dislike for countries which are associated with war (e.g. Iraq and Afghanistan), or which they see as historical enemies. Attitudes to the United States seem to be ambivalent as recorded in one large scale study (Reynolds and Vinterek, 2016), children were equally divided between liking it (fame factor) and disliking it (global dominance).

If a child in your class expressed a hatred for a nation and its peoples, how would you respond?

Is there any evidence that children's national preferences vary with age? Historical research by Jahoda (1962) suggests a developmental sequence in which the youngest children (six- to seven-year-olds) tended to favour exotic countries, children aged eight to nine preferred familiar countries such as holiday destinations, while ten- to eleven-year-olds referred to physical features or the character of the people to justify their opinions. More recently Tierney (2010) also noted a progression from simple stereotypes to more realistic and more complex understandings in a project in which young UK adolescents learnt about Sri Lanka. However, progression is neither consistent nor uniform. For example, a detailed study of a school linking project by Disney (2005) found a great range of responses within a group of children of the same age. In general terms it has been suggested that learning about other countries may be particularly well received in the junior years (ages seven to eleven) when children have moved beyond the egocentric orientation of early childhood and have developed a natural curiosity about other places and peoples (Scoffham, 2010). Further research is needed to establish this.

How children in Western industrialized countries view the global south (developing countries) is a particularly sensitive matter. Borowski (2011) found by using word association exercises and other studies that negative stereotypes are widespread and that many children hold an undifferentiated view of Africa which they regard as universally 'poor'. It appears that charity campaigns and emergency appeals compound these ideas by presenting graphic scenes of suffering and injustice (Oberman, 2014). Negative stereotypes, once formed, are difficult to dislodge because they serve as a 'lens' which colours further thinking. Schools can at least challenge these preconceptions by introducing alternative perspectives and exploring the reasons for global inequalities. The problem is that simply presenting and analysing information does not always change children's thinking as global learning taps into emotional as well as cognitive structures.

Can you think of any experiences or events that have changed your own ideas about another country?

The fact that learning about other countries and peoples is emotionally charged is one of its distinguishing features. People are fiercely protective of their own nation and strive to promote it in all sorts of ways. Around the world education is seen as a way of building a sense of national identity and it is common for children to begin the school day by taking some kind of oath of allegiance. In their lessons too, young people are introduced to the literature, art, music and other achievements which define their country in preference to those of other nations. The hidden meanings, associations and collective memories which pervade these 'texts' exert a powerful influence on children and adults alike. Furthermore, in the UK the focus on British values reinforces the idea that Britain is somehow different from other countries with its own traditions and distinctive way of life.

To what extent is this true in other countries?

Viewing these processes from the perspective of developmental psychology, Barrett (2007) concludes that global learning is 'emotionally hot' and that learning about other nations, peoples and cultures impacts on our sense of identity and challenges us to reflect on our relations with others. However, the fact that it is contentious is not a reason to ignore it. Quite the contrary. Schools have an important part to play in helping children develop balanced images of the world. Indeed, they may be the *only* place where children can access unbiased information and reflect constructively and creatively on the ideas that they hold. International perspectives are vital if people are to make sense of the ever more serious environmental issues which confront humanity and threaten to undermine the achievements of past centuries. The foundations of global understanding are laid at an early stage as children find out about places and peoples beyond their direct experience.

Further reading

Barrett, M. (2007) *Children's Knowledge, Beliefs and Feelings about Nations and National Groups*, Hove: Psychology Press.

Beneker, T., Tani, S., Uphues, R., and Van der Vart R. (2013) 'Young People's World-Mindedness and the Global Dimension in Their Geography Education: A Comparative Study of Upper Secondary School Students' Ideas in Finland, Germany and the Netherlands', *International Research in Geographical and Environmental Education*, 22, pp. 332–36.

Borowski, R. (2011) 'The Hidden Cost of a Red Nose', *Primary Geography*, 75, pp. 18–20.

Disney, A. (2005) 'Children's Images of a Distant Locality', *International Research in Geographical and Environmental Education*, 14:4, pp. 88–93.

Hennerdal, P. (2016) 'Changes in Place Location Knowledge: A Follow-up Study in Arvika, Sweden', *International Research in Geographical and Environmental Education*, 254, pp. 309–27.

Jahoda, G. (1962) 'Development of Scottish Children's Ideas and Attitudes about Other Countries', *Journal of Social Psychology*, 58, pp. 91–108.

Lowes, S. (2008) 'Mapping the World: Freehand Mapping and Children's Understanding of Geographical Concepts', *Research in Geographic Education*, 10:2, pp. 1–37.

Oberman, R., O'Shea, F., Hickey, B., and Joyce, C. (2014) *Children's Global Thinking*, Dublin: Education for a Just World.

Reynolds, R., and Vinterek, M. (2016) 'Geographical Locational Knowledge as an Indicator of Children's Views of the World: Research from Sweden and Australia', *International Research in Geographical and Environmental Education*, 25:1, pp. 68–83.

Scoffham, S. (2010) *Primary Geography Handbook*, Sheffield: Geographical Association.

Stillwell, R., and Spencer, C. (1973) 'Children's Early Preferences for Other Nations and Their Subsequent Acquisition of Knowledge about Those Nations', *European Journal of Social Psychology*, 3, pp. 354–49.

Tierney, M. (2010) 'Paradise on Earth or a Land of Many Problems?', *Teaching Geography*, 35:2, pp. 70–3.

Wiegand, P. (2006) *Learning and Teaching with Maps*, London: Routledge.

Part III

A meeting of minds

A perspective on the perspectives

The writers in Parts I and II have viewed aspects of educational practice from inside and outside their systems. In Part III educational issues in a range of countries are explored through a mixture of conversation, interviews and questioning. The chapters are aimed at stimulating debate about the influence of politics, policy, cultures and the needs of the children themselves, but also consider the impact of globalization and the interface between educational provision and the changing planetary environment.

22

How do we prepare teachers as global educators and balance national accreditation requirements with global challenges?

The issues around offering richly international teacher education programmes examined within the context of Ireland

Oliver McGarr

Teacher education in Ireland has undergone significant changes in the past decade and is now regulated by an independent statutory body, the Teaching Council of Ireland (O'Donoghue et al., 2017). This body sets out the regulations pertaining to initial teacher education and accredits teacher education programmes across the state. Prior to the establishment of the council, teacher education providers were accredited by the Department of

Education and Skills through a teachers' registration section; although the level of specificity in terms of programme requirements was not as detailed as current requirements. In that context teacher educators were afforded a high level of autonomy and significant programme variation existed across the many different teacher education colleges and universities. For example, the duration and timing of school placement experiences in both undergraduate concurrent teacher education programmes and postgraduate consecutive programmes varied significantly across the many providers and so too did their treatment of various aspects of education theory. This autonomy provided opportunities for a wide range of other student experiences reflecting institutional traditions and preferences, including alternative school placements and some overseas placements where overseas study and work experience could be given equivalent academic credits in the home institution.

Do you think Teacher Education should be autonomous?

The new criteria and guidelines in teacher education which have come into effect in recent years have resulted in a higher level of uniformity within the system. The new criteria and guidelines set out the various expectations in terms of programme content and European Credit Transfer and Accumulation System (ECTS) credit weighting. For example, they set out the required credit allocation of school placements on the programmes as well as their duration, the number of credits to be allocated to subject disciplines and the number of credits allocated to educational theory (Teaching Council, 2017). Within this latter area, further guidance is provided in terms of the areas of study required, for example, educational technology, sociology, educational psychology and so forth, and key learning outcomes are defined for such programmes. From a subject perspective there are detailed requirements for each curricular area that applicants to postgraduate initial teacher education programmes must provide evidence that they meet. These curricular requirements also determine the subject content of undergraduate concurrent teacher education programmes. For example, each subject area includes topics within the various subjects for which students must provide evidence that they have covered in their primary degrees. These must also meet minimum ECTS thresholds. To be considered for entry onto a postgraduate programme in initial teacher education to teach English at post-primary level, one's primary degree must cover a minimum of forty ECTS credits of literature in Drama, Poetry and Fiction as well as a minimum of twenty ECTS from 'optional' areas such as

Media Studies, Film Studies, Composition and Writing and Theatre Studies (Teaching Council, 2013).

What are the benefits and drawbacks of strict entry requirements?

While these guidelines have helped to provide a level of consistency across the teacher education landscape and indeed have sparked more long-term conversations in the teacher education community in Ireland, they have also created some unintended consequences. Among them is the narrowing of the potential pool of applicants due to the specificity in terms of suitable degree content. This has in effect reduced the number of 'suitable' primary degrees across many subject areas that enable entry into teacher education programmes. At a time when there are concerns about the homogeneity of the teaching profession (Keane and Heinz, 2015) it would seem contradictory to have entry criteria that further limit entry to the profession rather than widen it. This also comes at a time of concerns over teacher supply and the falling numbers of applicants applying for postgraduate programmes in teacher education nationally.

Another unintended consequence of the more recent reforms has been the effect on preparing teachers as global educators. In Ireland, teacher education, particularly at primary level, played a role in the 'nation building' project of the early state. Education was seen as an important device in defining and projecting a particular view of 'Irishness' through aspects such as compulsory Irish language classes for all pupils. Aspects of this focus continue to be evident today. Yet, as classrooms and communities become more culturally diverse through a more interconnected and global society, the need to prepare pupils as global citizens is more pressing than ever. Internationally this drive to add a global dimension to teacher education has manifest itself in incentives to open entry to the profession from groups not traditionally represented and encourage non-traditional entry routes to create greater diversity. International exchanges and study visits have also played an important role in ensuring that student teachers gain alternative perspectives on their own practices and school settings through comparing them with non-traditional sites of learning and international experiences.

In your view, what does a global dimension bring to a student's education?

Returning to the Irish context, the recent changes to criteria for registration have limited these opportunities. Accreditation compliance has made it more challenging to facilitate such international exchanges. As a result, while there is a recognition of the need for teachers to be aware of broader issues of social justice and equality, from not just a national perspective but also a global perspective, the reality for students can be quite different. Their teacher education programmes can remain exclusively focused on preparing teachers for Irish schools through placement in only Irish schools.

This contradiction highlights the tension between ensuring pre-service education is fit for purpose in preparing teachers for the challenges of schools in their local context while at the same time offering students a broader more global perspective to help them position their practice and professional work in a wider social and cultural global context. Donoghue et al. (2017) note that some of the influences that converged to bring about the current reforms in teacher education in Ireland included a move towards greater accountability for, and regulation of, teachers in the context of a lack of trust in the public sector. In such contexts one could argue that more 'parochial' concerns of the local trump more global needs. Whether this reflects a type of educational nimbyism at play or simply reflects the lack of awareness of the importance of providing teacher education with a global dimension is a matter for discussion. It may also reflect the evolutionary stage of development of teacher education in Ireland where local and national concerns dominate and more global challenges have not yet come to the fore.

To what extent does public and political pressure influence teacher education programmes and is there any 'wriggle room'?

The need to incorporate a global perspective into teacher education and more easily facilitate international placements as part of initial teacher education programmes is all the more pressing in the Irish system where the overwhelming majority of those entering the profession are white and from similar social class backgrounds. However, as Keane and Heinz (2015) note, this phenomenon is not unique to Ireland. Unless opportunities are included within these pre-service programmes for students to experience different cultures and settings, teacher education could become an exercise in conformity within a particular jurisdiction as opposed to an opportunity to challenge perspectives and interrogate prevailing mind-sets.

How could you quantify an international learning experience?

To address the current imbalance the teacher education community in Ireland must do more to advocate for such international placements. However, this is challenging in a culture of performativity where successful teaching education is increasingly seen as a narrow set of pedagogical competencies rather than as a more holistic understanding of human development. Teacher education must do more to provide evidence that such international placements not only capture the important learning outcomes of similar school-based placements in local schools, they must also show evidence that such placements achieve other learning outcomes that can be universally applied and relevant to all educational settings. Without such evidence it is unlikely that the current emphasis on practicum (the meeting national curriculum requirements) will be altered, given the current drives to more tightly regulate the profession.

Further reading

Keane, E., and Heinz, M. (2015) 'Diversity in Initial Teacher Education in Ireland: The Socio-Demographic Backgrounds of Postgraduate Post-Primary Entrants in 2013 and 2014', *Irish Educational Studies*, 34:3, pp. 281–301, DOI: 10.1080/03323315.2015.1067637.

O'Donoghue, T., Harford, J., and O'Doherty, T. (eds) (2017) 'Current Developments and Future Trends', in *Teacher Preparation in Ireland*, UK: Emerald, 207–25.

Teaching Council (2013) *Teaching Council Registration Curricular Subject Requirements (Post-Primary)*, Dublin: Teaching Council.

Teaching Council (2017) *Initial Teacher Education: Criteria and Guidelines for Programme Providers*, Dublin: Teaching Council.

23

How does prescribed curriculum content impact on inclusive education practices in emerging educational systems?

A researcher's perspective on inclusive education in post-apartheid South Africa

Viv Wilson and Mirna Nel

Since the publication of the Salamanca statement in 1994, inclusive education has developed as a global movement. This argues for the inclusion of all learners in mainstream education, regardless of their 'physical, intellectual, linguistic, social or other conditions' (UNESCO, 1994, p. 6). This statement resonated particularly strongly in South Africa, following the radical political changes taking place at the same time. The dismantling of apartheid and the introduction of democratic processes included a complete overhaul of the education system, with an emphasis on equity, respect for human dignity and human rights (Ministry of Education, 1995). Yet, there are many challenges to embedding inclusive education in the South African system.

This chapter raises the issue of balancing inclusive practices with a content-heavy, inflexible curriculum.

Dr Viv Wilson is a former principal lecturer based in the UK. She has acted as a consultant for education projects in Malaysia and Palestine as well as having wide-ranging experience of lecturing on Primary and Secondary Education programmes. Here she talks to Professor Mirna Nel from the Optentia Research Focus Area North-West University, South Africa (SA), who has extensive teaching, publishing and research expertise. Nel has published or co-published over twenty articles and book chapters related to inclusive practice in SA and is passionate about promoting the teacher's role in inclusive education.

Viv: Given the starting point for the South African education system in 1994 Mirna, what do you see as the biggest achievements regarding inclusive education?

Mirna: The emphasis on viewing inclusion as a human rights and social justice issue, not tolerating discrimination and respecting human dignity. We have such a poor history of human rights abuse in education, especially with regard to denying black children quality education and segregating children with disabilities from mainstream education that this needed to be a central focus of our inclusive education policies and practice. I also strongly believe that the social approach we follow as a foundational philosophy toward inclusive education is important. Our classrooms reflect a range of diversities with regard to race, gender, ethnicity, class, cultures, language, religion*, ability and disability, as well as learning needs. Consequently, I think that a predominant focus on the exclusion of children with disabilities alone can result in neglecting to address discriminatory actions based on the aforementioned differences. However, in the same breath I need to highlight the fact that the exclusion of children with disabilities should get more attention.

*[*South Africa has been called the 'rainbow nation' due to its multicultural population. There are eleven official languages and numerous ethnic groups.]*

Mirna: We also have a very strong legal basis, i.e. laws, policies and guideline documents. When presenting papers and lectures on inclusive education in South Africa internationally, peoples' immediate reaction is one of admiration for what we have achieved with our legal documents. This begins with our Constitution (1996a), the Schools' Act of 1996, and all the subsequent policies (such as Education White Paper 6, Department of Education, 2001) and guideline documents operationalizing inclusive education, which outline how we should teach, assess and support diverse learning needs in any classroom (e.g. Department of Basic Education, 2014).

I also need to mention the many schools, individuals, non-governmental organisations and activists that embraced inclusive education and continue to work very hard in making sure that teachers are enabled to teach in inclusive classrooms.

Viv: What do you see as the main challenges to the establishment of inclusive practice in South African schools?

Mirna: Most of the research in South Africa finds that our teachers believe inclusive education is the 'right thing' to do, despite all the challenges they experience. However, as always it is the transferral from beliefs and paper into practice.

In South Africa there are specific causes for this inaction of policy. Over the last two decades research has found numerous explanations for why the quality of our education system in general is rated as one of the poorest in the world. However, I want to highlight a key obstacle that I believe needs to be addressed urgently by government in order to help all educationists (in schools and universities) enact inclusive education. I am referring to the content driven, 'curriculum coverage' approach that is enforced by the education department.

A fundamental principle of inclusive education, which is emphasized in our policies, is a flexible curriculum to ensure all learners' learning pace and needs are addressed to consequently achieve successful *learning* i. e. a learner-centred, constructive curriculum. However, currently teachers and learners are driven to complete a prescribed curriculum, meaning the content has to be dealt with in a certain amount of time, memorized and regurgitated in the test and exam to ascertain good average pass percentages. Our education system can therefore be described as content-and-results driven. As one teacher puts it 'It is about quantity and not quality'. Besides resulting in parrot education, this does not allow for learners who experience barriers to learning in the mainstream classes to keep-up with their peers. In addition to the curriculum coverage demands, with large classroom numbers (in many cases up to fifty pupils and more), teachers believe that they do not have the training, knowledge, skills and time to teach and support these learners.

Mirna: As a result, a medical-deficit approach is still applied, where learners are referred, labelled, categorized and placed into special education, in many instances unfairly. Based on our current research in schools (Grosser, Nel, Kloppers and Esterhuizen, in process) a number of learners are wrongly labelled as 'slow' learners because of systemic reasons, such as the application of an inflexible curriculum, or learning in a second language, as well as inefficient support structures and systems.

Viv. In your opinion, what would make the biggest difference to the development of inclusive practice in South Africa?

Mirna: Firstly, by ending the practice of politicians using education results for their own political agendas by putting the focus on average pass percentages and comparing schools' results. More importantly, by refraining from overemphasizing the learning of content and instead implementing a flexible, constructive curriculum promoting a focus on the learning process and the development of critical thinking skills.

This requires us to go back to where we started with inclusive education, to re-assess existing systemic, contextual, environmental and social barriers. This socio-ecological approach is integral to successful inclusive practices.

Mirna: This re-assessment is crucial to stop applying a behaviouristic approach to education, as well as the deficit-within-child model. Furthermore, training *all* teacher educators, pre-service and in-service teachers as well as departmental officials on how to understand and apply an inclusive pedagogy, but also putting in place a good mentoring and support system to ensure that it is appropriately enacted.

Viv: What do you consider to be the most important lessons from the South African experience for other countries?

Mirna: As mentioned earlier our legal and guideline documents provide a good foundation for the approach and structuring of the education system in providing inclusive education. However, in the process of transforming our education system it seems that the central focus on the child and how he/ she develops got lost, as well as the belief that every child deserves the kind of education that ensures successful learning. There remains a gap between how government regards the purpose of education and how educationists (including researchers) can actually bring policies and practices nearer to each other.

The key lesson that can consequently be learned from South Africa is that constructive, collaborative partnerships between all stakeholders (including learners, parents/caregivers, teachers, teacher educators, researchers, community members, departmental officials, politicians and business people) are critical to ensure that systemic, socio-environmental and contextual factors are continuously evaluated, but essentially remembering that the child's learning and development should be at the centre of it all.

Questions to consider

Nel contrasts inclusion viewed as a social justice issue with inclusion viewed mainly in terms of special educational needs. Where do you stand in your definition of inclusive education, and why?

From your own experience, can you identify existing barriers to inclusive education under Nel's four headings? You might find it useful to consider the work of Bronfenbrenner (1994).

Nel suggests that the official attitude to the school curriculum affects teachers' beliefs about inclusive education. Why might this be the case? How would you compare, or contrast this with the situation in other countries?

How important do you think educational policies are in developing and sustaining inclusive classrooms? What other factors might also be important?

The practice of 'labelling' learners may not be so obvious in all countries, but it does occur. Can you think of any examples from your own experience? In what ways might this disadvantage these pupils?

The idea of learner-centred education has been central to Nel's argument throughout this interview. What does this philosophy mean to you, and how easy is it in your education system?

Further reading

Bronfenbrenner, U. (1994) 'Ecological Models of Human Development', *Readings on the Development of Children*, 2:1, pp. 37–43.

Department of Basic Education (2014) *Policy on Screening, Identification, Assessment and Support* (SIAS), Pretoria: Sol Plaatjie House.

Department of Education (DoE) (2001) *Education White Paper 6: Special Needs Education. Building an Inclusive Education and Training System*, Pretoria: Department of Education.

Grosser, M., Nel, M., Kloppers, M., and Esterhuizen, S. (In process) *Teacher Readiness towards Achieving Advanced Performance among All Learners.*

Ministry of Basic Education (1995) *White Paper on Education and Training in a Democratic South Africa: First Steps to Develop a New System*, Pretoria: Sol Plaatjie House.

Republic of South Africa (RSA) (1996a) *Constitution (Act 108 of 1996)*, Pretoria: Sol Plaatjie House.

Republic of South Africa (1996b) *South African Schools Act 84 of 1996*, Pretoria: Sol Plaatjie House.

UNESCO (1994) The Salamanca Statement and Framework for Action http://www.unesco.org/education/pdf/SALAMA_E.PDF (Accessed February 2018).

24

What are the challenges for teachers of implementing curriculum change?

A discussion of the new curriculum in Palestine and how it has been received by teachers

Hanan Jibril-Dabdoub, Maria Elsam and Joy Mower

Hanan Jibril-Dabdoub from the National Institute of Education and Training, Palestine, Maria Elsam and Joy Mower from Canterbury Christ Church University, UK, worked together on the Teacher Education Improvement Project in the Occupied Palestinian Territories of the West Bank and Gaza. Jibril – Dabdoub is a training supervisor at the National Institute of Educational Training. Within this role she is the co-ordinater for component 2 of the World Bank Teacher Education Improvement Project in Palestine, focused on upgrading competencies and skills of under-qualified teachers from grade 1–4. She has extensive experience as a teacher in schools and as a university lecturer; her professional interests and expertise include curriculum development and innovation in teaching and learning. Drawing on an interview and discussion, this chapter reflects Jibril-Dabdoub's perceptions of the current situation regarding curriculum change in Palestine. National educational outcomes, measured and compared internationally, prompt questions about effectiveness of curricula and pedagogy, often generating changes in policy. In this chapter we discuss who and what initiated change in the West Bank Palestinian Occupied Territory. Jibril-Dabdoub provides insight into how the envisioned changes to the curriculum and perceptions about effective pedagogy have translated into practice.

Prior to 1994 Palestinian children in the West Bank were taught using the Jordanian curriculum while the schools in Gaza used the Egyptian Curriculum (Mulkeen, 2013). Following the Oslo Accords of 1993 and the establishment of the Palestinian Authority in the West Bank Occupied Territories, the need was identified to create a Palestinian Curriculum, reflecting national identity and requirements. Teachers and supervisors worked collaboratively with experts from the Ministry of Education and Higher Education (MoEHE, 2014); it was seen as patriotic work. As global educational systems of assessment and comparison gained significance internationally the MoEHE had become concerned about Palestine's poor results and low position (TIMSS, 2011). The belief was that to develop the nation, the curriculum also needed developing, and updating, and that new ways of teaching were needed. Whilst maintaining a strong sense of national identity within the content, Palestine looked to the rest of the world, tried to identify what was effective practice and to assimilate it within a revised curriculum.

How has the change to the curriculum in Palestine also demanded a change to the pedagogical approach in Palestinian classrooms?

In Palestine, the traditional view of teaching is that the focus is on the teacher. Palestinian teachers work from textbooks. With a revised curriculum new textbooks had to be written and implemented quickly; workshops for district supervisors and teachers were held to inform them of the changes and the new requirements. The new view is to focus on the student and their needs, on embedding technology in classrooms, on interaction and communication: '21st century skills' (Trilling and Fadel, 2009). The new textbooks have less content than previously and are more activity-led. For teachers, they are the 'curriculum in action'. But teachers are not finding it easy, as previously the textbooks were very detailed in providing all the necessary content to be taught and the teacher's role was to 'deliver' this. The curriculum still encompasses a wide range of content, but the textbook is less prescriptive in setting out exactly how everything should be taught. It is no longer considered enough to have an understanding of the subject being taught, the necessary content knowledge, but also of teaching and learning processes, pedagogical knowledge and how to bring these together appropriately: pedagogical content knowledge, 'the ways of representing and formulating the subject that make it comprehensible to others' (Shulman, 1986, p. 9). The emphasis in the past was on what was taught rather than outcomes for individual children. The aim is to develop a more learner-centred approach and the activities in the text book are designed to support this.

What are the processes being employed in Palestine to bring about curriculum change?

Once the need for a revised curriculum was identified and it had been designed, there was a political and logistical need to implement it quickly, so materials also had to be produced at speed to be in place in Palestinian classrooms at the start of the new academic year. Whereas the curriculum itself was written by the MoEHE, the textbooks were written by teams of education professionals including those working for the National Institute of Education and Training (NIET) and for the Department of Supervision and Qualifications (DSQ). Unlike with the 1994 curriculum, teachers were not involved in the development, due to the pressure of time. For each subject taught, there are currently two textbooks, one covering the content for the first semester and another for the second semester. Meetings at which the textbooks were introduced were held shortly before the start of each semester; the second set of textbooks were not ready at the start of the year. Many of the district supervisors, who, along with the school principals, oversee the work of the teachers, were trained alongside the teachers. The training focused on the content of the textbook, rather than the values and philosophy of the curriculum. Teachers were unhappy because they felt unsupported. They believe they are still required to teach the full content as previously, but the more activity-led approach of the new textbooks provides a different type of framework, one which demands more planning and decision-making on their part. This has highlighted issues around teachers' confidence with this approach and their concerns about the way in which they are assessed.

The Palestinian Authority have also looked to external agencies to address some of the perceived issues with education in Palestine; the World Bank-funded Teacher Education Improvement Project (TEIP, World Bank Org., 2018) has provided further professional development for approximately two thousand in-service teachers. TEIP has promoted a learner-centred approach and teachers who have graduated from the project, have demonstrated a greater awareness of learners and learning and a desire to use the textbook more creatively and flexibly. Teachers have also developed their own informal support networks, often through social media, perhaps using the very skills that the curriculum is trying to develop in the children. Through these informal networks, plans and resources can be shared easily, although discussion of theory and underpinning pedagogical ideas has so far been limited. The support networks are currently perceived as serving a more practical function, possibly filling the confidence gap of 'how to', left by the previous textbooks. Although teachers feel they are doing this from necessity, perhaps this has developed a collegiate and collaborative culture that is bottom up, rather than top down.

What barriers are there to realizing, in Palestinian classrooms, the original vision and philosophy underpinning the curriculum change?

Within a socio-ecological understanding of the relationship between an individual and their environment (Bronfenbrenner, 1979), there are layers of cultural influence that interact with each other and within which the individual acts and these are the context in which they learn and develop. The teachers in Palestine were asked to embed a new curriculum, as presented in the new textbooks, and their understanding and development, as well as barriers to these, can be analysed in the context of a socio-ecological, layered system.

Teachers' own upbringing and education and their perceptions and beliefs about what it means to be a teacher may be one of the overriding influences on their practice. Palestinian teachers are often deeply invested in their identity as a teacher, as they perceive it as highly patriotic for demonstrating their commitment and belief in their Palestinian heritage and future. The culture in a teacher's school, the specific routines, expectations and requirements also influence a teacher's understanding of what constitutes 'good practice' and their perception of their own effectiveness. This might reflect their relationship with the school principal and district supervisor, both of whom have a role in observing and assessing teachers. The quality of their teaching has traditionally been judged largely on their ability to deliver the content of the textbook and teachers are now unsure about how new pedagogical approaches will be viewed and the implications for external assessment of their practice. Teachers are assessed by standards set by the Commission for Developing the Teaching Profession (CDTP). The manner in which these are applied may impact on teachers' behaviour and the enactment of the curriculum. Palestinian teachers' perception of their role often leans more towards that of a technician than of an autonomous professional.

Policy changes that require teachers to change the ways in which they think about teaching and learning and that create more demands on a teacher's time and effort are difficult to embed without teachers developing an understanding of the underlying values and philosophy. Evidence from the TEIP project suggests that curriculum change is apparent where teachers have had additional professional development and support in school from principals and supervisors who encourage them to be creative and innovative leaders of change.

Questions to consider

What are the barriers to and the consequences of change for teacher?

To make curriculum change effective, what, ideally, would be the role of the different stakeholders in its implementation and development?

Can you identify what may have initiated curriculum change within your own context? To what extent are global comparisons and economic forces the drivers? Are concepts of national identity apparent and what role do they play?

Consider the 'ecology' of teachers' classroom practice. What are the different 'cultural layers' that influence and direct teachers' practice? Where might there be tensions with these?

In your own curriculum is there a tension between content and application? How can this be resolved?

What is the relationship between what is taught and how it is taught? Does the curriculum dictate or suggest a particular pedagogical approach?

Further reading

Bronfenbrenner, U. (1979) *The Ecology of Human Development*, Cambridge: Harvard University Press.

CDTP, Hashweh, M. (2011) *Teacher Education Strategy: Review of Implementation Status*, Palestine Ministry of Education and Higher Education at: https://www.amideast.org/sites/default/files/otherfiles/msn/MSN_TeacherEducationStrategy.pdf. (Accessed November 12, 2018).

Ministry Of Education and Higher Education (2014) Education Development Strategic Plan (EDSP): A Learning Nation at: http://planipolis.iiep.unesco.org/sites/planipolis/files/ressources/palestine_education_development_strategic_plan_2014_2019.pdf (Accessed February 2018).

Mulkeen, A. (2013) *Consultancy to the Palestinian Authority Ministry of Education to Support the Development of a Plan for Curriculum Reform*, Draft Report, 20 April 2013.

Oslo Accords (1993) Information on the Oslo Accords can be accessed at: https://www.globalpolicy.org/component/content/article/189-israel-palestine/38356-the-oslo-accords.html. (Accessed March 2018).

Ozga, J., and Lingard, B. (2006) 'Globalisation, Education Policy and Politics', in Ozga, J., and Lingard, R. (eds), *The Routledge Reader in Education Policy and Politics*, London: Routledge, pp. 65–82.

Shulman, L. (1986) 'Those Who Understand: Knowledge Growth in Teaching', *Educational Researcher*, 15:2, pp. 4–14.

Thomson, P., Lingard, B., and Wrigley, T. (2012) 'Reimagining School Change', in Wrigley, T., Thomson, P., and Lingard, B. (eds), *Changing Schools: Alternative Ways to Make a World of Difference*, London: Routledge, pp. 1–14.

TIMSS (Trends in International Mathematics and Science Study) (2011) A guide to TIMSS 2011 can be found at: https://timssandpirls.bc.edu/timss2011/international-database.html (Accessed March 2018).

Trilling, B., and Fadel, C. (2009) *21st Century Skills: Learning for Life in Our Times*, San Francisco: Wiley/Jossey-Bass.

World Bank (2018) 'Projects and Operations', in *Teacher Education Improvement Project*, at: http://projects.worldbank.org/P111394/teacher-education-improvement-project?lang=en (Accessed February 2018).

25

What can be gained from intercultural engagements?

Bridging the cultural divide between students in southern India and UK student teachers

Christudas Amala Lal and Simon Hoult

Learning about oneself through understanding the cultural 'Other' is an important desirable outcome from the study abroad interactions between our students from South India and the UK. However, study abroad to the 'global south' has also often failed to expose the 'western' epistemology that underpins the thinking of those from the 'global north' (Martin, 2011). We begin with the premise, nevertheless, that through intercultural engagements deep learning *may* occur with the potential for this to inform and change ourselves personally and professionally. In this chapter we consider what can be gained from intercultural engagements during a sojourn to Kerala, South India, by students based in Canterbury, UK with particular focus on our reflections on a conference involving both UK and Indian students. We recognize that within such a short chapter it is not possible to focus more broadly and for a consideration of the participant voice from this sojourn please see Hoult and Lal (2015) and Hoult (2018).

The conference at the University of Kerala entitled *Bridging the Gaps: Education, Language and Culture* held in 2014, brought together student teachers and other scholars primarily from the University of Kerala, the Government College of Teacher Education, Thiruvananthapuram and Canterbury Christ Church University, UK. The conference focused on our common disciplines of English and education set within the context of the cultures within which we live, study and work.

The conference enabled students to present their scholarly endeavours as well as critically reflect about their practice in teaching English in Kerala, and more generally primary and secondary teaching in England. Crucially, it enabled students to interact with one another about their lives as young people, scholars and emerging professionals in Kerala and the UK. The interactions perhaps provoked more complex and nuanced understandings of the educational culture of the 'Other' that recognized differences, but also identified similarities within a modern and changing global context. Consequent to these interactions and ensuing intercultural learning, students not only learnt about other approaches to education, but also potentially began to imagine different futures for themselves.

What do you understand by the terms 'intercultural' and 'Other' in the context of experiencing different cultures?

Any engagement with peers from a different culture is never a neutral act. Events like conferences, and the relationships and pedagogical debates that potentially ensue, have strong political and power dimensions that are 'written through' these experiences. To *some* degree we live in political, and to a lesser extent economic, postcolonial times, yet, as Wa Thiong'o (1986) argues, 'decolonising the mind' is on ongoing struggle. Accordingly, an intention of the sojourn was that such an exposure, and the realization of the extent to which we are *all* written through with the colonial, had the potential for this to challenge and change our worldviews. We liken this process to transformational learning, should this challenge cause an epistemological change in the learner (Mezirow, 2000). The *Bridging the Gaps* conference provided the opportunity for *all* students to reconsider theory and practice related to English language teaching specifically and education more widely, as well as deeper aspects about themselves from their interactions with the 'Other'.

How might the inclusion of theory in the discussions alter the way that students engaged with one another?

Cosmopolitan imaginations

Our social actions and decisions happen in complex situations where their outcomes are uncertain but often have global determining factors (Delanty, 2009). Our psychological interpretations of these factors mean that we all consider matters differently, albeit within dominant cultural paradigms. A cosmopolitan orientation and attitude towards our social actions and decision making provide a means to express and interpret our world experiences. The cosmopolitan experience and interpretation of the 'Other' through a reinterpretation of the 'Self' is called the Cosmopolitan Imagination (Delanty, 2009). This imagination is provoked during 'moments of openness' to develop a new relationship between 'Self' and 'Other' in a world setting (2009, p. 53), which we hope included during our *Bridging the Gaps* conference.

In what situations might 'moments of openness' be best developed in yourself, and how might this influence the way you consider yourself and the 'Other'?

A cosmopolitan imagination has the potential to provide a context within which to consider the conference participants' changing views through their intercultural interactions as well as indicating a means by which transformative learning takes place. One's imagination is important in an intercultural setting; the ability to imagine other viewpoints is a significant dimension to transformative learning (Mezirow, 2000). Delanty (2009, p. 7) identifies four social orientations that enable a cosmopolitan imagination to develop. A cosmopolitan orientation:

1 Stresses cultural difference and pluralization.
2 Occurs in the context of global–local relations.
3 Thinks beyond established borders.
4 Involves the reinvention of political community around global ethics.

The emphasis on the ability to think beyond borders helps alleviate essentialism, which produces a potentially nationalistic othering, defining the 'Other' through a 'grossly simplistic exaggerated and homogenous, imagined, single culture' (Holliday, 2011, p. 5). In contrast, cosmopolitan imagining has the potential to transcend the danger of national identities dictating our worldview in a search for a more global scale of intercultural communication and transformation (Holliday, 2011). The danger in bringing students from two countries together was that it potentially reinforced a 'them' and 'us' culture by merely comparing at a national level 'what we do here' with 'what they do there'. However, the conference's focus on the students' common areas of study and in many cases future profession, meant that learning seemed to transcend simple comparative national levels and moved towards seeing commonalities and differences at a professional 'lived' level between fellow education professionals and scholars.

During a visit when many experiences were expected to be different from 'home', why do you think the students deemed connecting with fellow students so important?

Dispositions towards intercultural learning

The spaces that the *Bridging the Gaps* conference provided enabled the Keralan and UK students to interact with one another in a relatively informal conference atmosphere. The presentations provided stimuli for conversations between students during breaks. These were powerful opportunities for intercultural exchanges, enabling open and fluid dispositions towards intercultural learning to emerge, redolent of some of the higher 'Learning Spaces' developed by Andreotti (2010). Andreotti outlines seven learning spaces with the first exemplifying thinking that is singular, certain and fixed, to space seven that embraces complexity and conflicting opinion. In the seventh space learners understand that our responses are highly contextualized and change as situations alter. It is in the higher learning spaces that our thinking can support a cosmopolitan imagination and potentially transformative learning. It was such nuanced understandings that we hoped our students would attain from the conference where learning was developed within a global context. Andreotti (2010) emphasizes the social construction of 'provisional meaning' (2010, p. 16) and the deepening of analysis that occurs in these uncertain spaces. These learning spaces seem to concur with her epistemological position where 'knowledge, learning, reality and identities [are] socially constructed, fluid, open to negotiation and always provisional' (2010, p. 6).

To what extent does thinking about local experiences in a global context alter your thoughts?

We begin to see the importance of the fluid space that the conference provided when we regard our ability to learn in different spaces as partly dependent on the context of that learning, rather than something that is fixed or concrete. The context of learning includes our perceptions of the place where that learning is situated, the nature of the new knowledge being presented, the pedagogies employed and our disposition towards such contexts. Such a local context is important, notwithstanding the influences of macro-scale societal hegemonies. Hegemonies can be challenged through personal psychological micro-factors which are more time and space dependent, including variables such as confidence, adaptability and resilience all linked to previous experiences, or our 'hauntings' (Frosh, 2013), which return in various conscious and unconscious ways to influence our thinking and actions at different times and places.

If we assume that humans perform across a range of learning spaces, it may be the case that when an individual's experience is perceived to be too traumatic they retreat to an entrenched position. Of course, the opposite is also possible. A constructive and open, rather than defensive, response to new experiences may be engineered through the pedagogical environment that is developed; something we sought through the conference ambience. In order to support our students in developing an open approach to their learning we aimed to generate a safe space to speak and to question, where mutual learning through co-construction was the dominant dimension to the intercultural exchanges. Such learning concurs with Bruner's (1990) views on open-mindedness as 'a willingness to construe knowledge and values from multiple perspectives without loss of commitments to one's own values' (cited by Mezirow, 2000, p. 13). A pluralist view associated with the open, fluid dimensions of 'learning space seven' and the cosmopolitan imagination discussed earlier hints at transformative intercultural learning through the development of open and inclusive frames of reference (discussed in our other publications).

What sorts of environment and engagement do you think develops an open and fluid approach between ourselves and the 'Other' and conversely can we still change when our disposition to the 'Other' is more singular and fixed?

In conclusion, this short reflection on the *Bridging the Gaps* conference has highlighted the importance of approaching such events with an explicit agenda to deepen intercultural learning as well as share ideas related to the focus of the conference. Drawing on the literature around intercultural and transformative learning helped us develop this agenda, as did an overall underpinning of postcolonial theory. The success of the conference in deepening intercultural learning arose from the conversations that it provoked in an open, constructive manner. It was significant that the common scholarly and professional fields of English and learning to teach provided a means to transcend simplistic national boundaries and to forge connections between students that lasted far longer than the duration of the conference.

Acknowledgements

This chapter is adapted from Hoult, S., and Lal, C. A. (2015) 'Introduction: Negotiating intercultural Learning Spaces', in Hoult, S., and Lal, C. A. (eds), *Bridging the Gaps: Critical Reflections on Intercultural Learning*, Trivandrum: Bodhi Tree Books.

Further reading

Andreotti, V. (2010) 'Global Education in the 21st Century: Two Different Perspectives on the "Post-" of Postmodernism', *International Journal of Development Education and Global Learning*, 2:2, pp. 5–22.

Andreotti, V. (2013) 'Taking Minds to Other Places', *Primary Geographer*, Spring 2013, Geographical Association, pp. 12–13.

Bruner, J. (1990) *Acts of Meaning*, Cambridge: Harvard University Press.

Delanty, G. (2009) *The Cosmopolitan Imagination: The Renewal of Critical Social Theory*, Cambridge: Cambridge University Press.

Frosh, S. (2013) *Hauntings: Psychoanalysis and Ghostly Transmissions*, London: Palgrave.

Holliday, A. (2011) *Intercultural Communication and Ideology*, London: Sage.

Hoult, S. (2018) 'Aspiring to a Postcolonial Engagement with the Other: Deepening Intercultural Learning through Reflection on a South Indian Sojourn', in Jackson, J., and Oguro, S. (eds), *Intercultural Interventions in Study Abroad*, London: Routledge.

Martin, F. (2011) 'Global Ethics, Sustainability and Partnership', in Butt, G. (ed.), *Geography, Education and the Future*, London: Bloomsbury, pp. 206–24.

Mezirow, J. (2000) 'Learning to Think like an Adult: Core Concepts of Transformation Theory', in Mezirow, J. (ed.), *Learning as Transformation: Critical Perspectives on a Theory in Progress*, San Francisco: Jossey Bass.

Wa Thiong'o, N. (1986) *Decolonising the Mind: The Politics of Language in African Literature*, Oxford: James Curry.

26

How might experiencing another culture challenge assumptions?

How living and working in China enabled an 'expert' educator to reflect on Early Childhood Education

Clair Stevens with Sue Hammond

China's immense market growth and industrial power has led the country to become one of the world's leading twenty-first century economies. The wealth generated by this burgeoning economy has led to the emergence of a new Chinese middle class who travel to different parts of the world, experiencing different lifestyles, beliefs and attitudes (Rocca, 2017). These experiences have, in turn, resulted in increased parental interest in preschool education with an emphasis on 'providing quality ECE' (Early Childhood Education) and quality kindergarten teachers (Rao, Zhou and Sun, 2017, p. 60). Educationalists from China have visited a range of ECE provision across the world, including Finland, Italy and England, seeking ideas for structuring their own early years' education.

Nursery Director Clair Stevens led one of the nurseries in England approached by groups of representatives from early years' providers in China. After Stevens' nursery received the Nursery World 'Nursery of the Year' award in 2014, interest from China grew immensely. The Chinese owners and managers who visited ran various private nurseries and kindergartens across China. They were impressed by the many ways that the nursery involved young children in the outside environment and the wider community. They were equally impressed, however, by Stevens' academic qualifications and the value she assigned to ensuring all nursery employees had knowledge of child development and early years' pedagogy, with an explicit emphasis on play.

These initial visits to the setting in England paved the way for a number of future contracts that involved working in China. The longest was for a period of four months in Guangzhou where Stevens was employed as a Foreign Director working with a new Forest School nursery. In the Guangzhou nursery, play was treated as an essential part of children's everyday lives until they entered statutory schooling at age six to seven years. Interestingly, this coincided with a shift in policy discourse around early years' education in England from an emphasis on play and development to an ideology underpinned by notions of 'school readiness' (DfE, 2014). Rather than valuing this period of young children's lives for the learning opportunities and experiences it offers, the approach being promoted by the DfE in England (DfE, 2014) implied that preschool education was primarily aimed at preparing young children for formal schooling. The main issue at the centre of this chapter, therefore, is on perceptions of quality in ECE.

What does 'quality' early childhood education mean to you?

The Chinese nursery owners with whom Stevens worked were keen to respond to parental concerns about city pollution, children's screen-time, unhealthy eating and lack of physical activity. They wanted young children to connect to nature and to care about their environment. Although Guangzhou was booming, its industrialization meant that environmental topographies such as a blue sky or stars were seldom visible. Although many nurseries and kindergartens in the cities had limited outdoor space, even the space that was available was not necessarily integrated into daily use. Moreover, the teachers who worked with the children were well qualified, many to masters' level, but had no knowledge of child development or early years' pedagogy. Many teachers felt ill-equipped to deal with the youngest children.

These characteristics were in stark contrast to the Anji Kindergarten Play Education in eastern China, introduced by Cheng Xueqin in 2001. As well as changing practice in one hundred and twenty-eight public preschools across China, it has since been adopted by Wisconsin in the United States and attracted international interest (Coffino, 2017). In Anji Play kindergartens children are free to explore outside using natural resources, especially designed materials, and cultural artefacts which are often created from locally sourced bamboo or clay (Anji Play, 2018). They are provided with flexible environments in which they can be independent, innovative and imaginative. The children are also expected to keep the spaces tidy and to take responsibility for their surroundings. Their teachers' role is to observe the play and learning and to play alongside the children, to 'Encourage and support risk, working with one another, finding solutions, and self-pacing' (Anji Play, 2018). The children's morning play activities are frequently videoed and played back to them later in the day. These 'play stories' provide them with opportunities to reflect on or re-tell their play narratives, with the potential of enriching and recognizing their experiences. Anji Play is a curriculum and ideology defined by clearly articulated principles, such as love, risk-taking, self-determination and delight in learning.

In what ways does the Anji Play philosophy resonate with other approaches to ECE?

For Stevens, changing practice in Guangzhou nurseries and kindergartens was also guided by a set of principles, but underpinned by the core value that change has to be respectful of local context and cultural traditions. While her remit included training the teachers about child development, she also built relationships with them, found out about their abilities and talents. For instance, most of the teachers were accomplished musicians and many spoke good English. They primarily lacked knowledge about the important part that authentic, first-hand experiences have on children's language and development. These can be exciting, extraordinary events but they can also be about closer looking in everyday contexts, about being a partner in a child's learning, helping them to build narratives or to extend their use of available resources. Before Stevens' arrival, the teachers worked with structured planning and themes that left little room for children's interests or fascinations.

When have you observed a child's learning or involvement in play being extending by sensitive interaction by an adult?

Encouraging the Guangzhou teachers and children to interact in the outdoor environment provided numerous opportunities. There was an abundance of fruit trees to explore and find out about. For example, there were lychees to touch, to taste and to breathe in their aroma in the tropical, humid climate. There were bananas to look at day by day, to examine and observe their growth and to evaluate when they were suitable for harvesting and eating. There were plants and other trees to study and find out about; 'China has 7,000 species of woody plants', including 'the metasequoia, China cypress, cathaya, silver fir, Fujian cypress, and eucommia' which do not grow elsewhere (Embassy of the People's Republic of China, 2018).

The participants, young and old, collaborated and shared in these simple pleasures, becoming more attuned to the wonders of the natural world and perhaps to the threats that challenge its preservation; indeed, conservation is a wider concern of the Chinese government. Involvement from the children was often observed in sensory exploration, an aspect that was incorporated into the training for teachers. The children, ranging from ages three to seven years, were often found in the forest, playing with the water pump, digging for insects, climbing trees or building dens.

Stevens has powerful memories of cooking on open fires with traditional ingredients and foraging fruit, vegetables and spices. These brought wonderful aromas to the camp and the children were encouraged to be involved at every stage. They washed fruit and vegetables, prepared, seasoned and tasted new dishes. Previously, the teachers had not considered these as 'learning opportunities' and therefore much of this preparation had occurred away from the children.

From small beginnings in your own environment, how can children and adults become custodians of the world's limited resources?

Raising awareness of ecological issues has become a key influence on the curriculum in many countries. Stevens' capacity to excite children and adults about the environment was a motivating factor for the private nurseries in Guangzhou to employ her. After harnessing the children's delight in being outdoors, it was possible to also involve their parents and even their grandparents in various events. These included growing food, preparing it and sitting together to enjoy it as a community.

Though grandparents have traditionally cared for their grandchildren in China, since the spread of ECE they have become responsible instead for taking and collecting their grandchildren from nursery. Stevens recognized the important contribution grandparents could make to children's, and indeed other adults', awareness of traditional and community culture. Their local knowledge extended beyond feasts, festivals and fashions, the tokenistic view of cultures that English schools have been criticized for promoting (Meyer and Rhoades, 2006). Grandparents were able to share their rich cultural knowledge of tales and songs, often communicated through rituals, folklore and personal family stories. With the involvement of parents and grandparents alongside the nursery staff, the children learnt how to dye materials to create the vibrant red used in many Chinese celebrations, or listened to traditional stories and tales that often involved shadow play and music.

These experiences were exhilarating for the children and adults alike, enriching the children's lives through first-hand experiences. Stevens gradually realized that her main contribution was not in sharing or transporting a pre-existing model of European practice. By sharing her excitement in the unfamiliar, teachers and families were reminded of the possibilities that already existed in their communities and culture, became acquainted with ways of making these relevant to the present and to the future through their children.

What is the importance of intergenerational family narratives? How might these contribute to a sense of belonging, connection and responsibility?

In reflecting on the diverse challenges and rewards of her experience in China, Stevens acknowledged that each day impacted on her own learning. She had been particularly surprised by the lack of pressure there was on the children to perform in certain ways or to achieve preset goals. Parents and educators seemed more interested in a child's ability to think creatively, in offering numerous opportunities to play using traditional materials such as sand, water or clay, or developing skills in woodworking, sewing and drawing.

There was one other key area that was important to parents and families and that was language and communication, in particular learning English. This was held in high regard and parents wanted daily English classes taught in a formal way. Nevertheless, through discussion and negotiation with families, opportunities to use the English language in context were built into play experiences throughout each day. Hearing the language and engaging in fun, playful interactions with teachers with whom they had developed strong, positive relationships gave robust foundations for linguistic growth. Perhaps the children's excitement in learning English was a more powerful indicator of their progress than any test or developmental milestone could reveal.

Further reading

Anji Play (2018) *The Fundamental Rights and Responsibilities of True Play*, Available at: http://www.anjiplay.com/rights (Accessed April 2018).

Cheng Xueqin (2015) *The Politics of True Play with Cheng Xueqin*. Vialogue available at: https://vialogues.com/vialogues/play/20933/ (Accessed April 2018).

Coffino, J. (2017) *How Did 'Anji Play' Go Global?* Available at: https://medium.com/@AnjiPlay/how-did-anji-play-go-global-18e1e4bca996 (Accessed March 2018).

Department for Education (2014) *Helping Disadvantaged Children Start School*. Available at: https://www.gov.uk/government/publications/are-you-ready-good-practice-in-school-readiness (Accessed May 2018).

Embassy of the People's Republic of China in Australia (2018) *China Flora and Fauna*. Available at: http://au.china-embassy.org/eng/zggk/t46173.htm (Accessed April 2018).

Meyer, C., and Rhoades, E. (2006) 'Multiculturalism: Beyond Food, Festival, Folklore, and Fashion', *Kappa Delta Pi Record*, 42:2, pp. 82–7.

Rao, N., Zhou, J., and Sun, J. (eds) (2017) *Early Childhood Education in Chinese Societies*, Netherlands: Springer Science.

Rocca, J.-L. (2017) *The Making of the Chinese Middle Class: Small Comfort and Great Expectations*, New York: Palgrave Macmillan.

27

How can we learn to live within planetary limits?

As environmental changes increasingly affect our daily lives, ways are suggested of educating children without filling them with fear

Stephen Scoffham with Margaret Sangster

You have a special brief to promote sustainability within education. Why is it so important for children to learn about sustainability?

The children who are at school today are set to inherit a world which is going through dramatic changes. Since the 1950s, world population has more or less trebled, energy use has quadrupled and economic activity (Gross Domestic Product or GDP) has increased sevenfold.

Economic development has brought great benefits but it has also brought great responsibilities. For the first time in history, humanity has obtained the power to alter the balance of life on Earth. Pollution and environmental stress have become pressing problems. It is now established, for example, that increasing levels of atmospheric carbon dioxide are causing irreversible global climate change. Also, around the world soils and natural habitats have been degraded and there has been a widespread collapse of plant and animal life. Scientists have even begun to recognize that human activity is a force of geological significance and they have coined the term 'anthropocene' to characterize the current era.

How can children comprehend such big issues?

Teaching children about sustainability is no simple matter. On the one hand it is all too easy to present gloom-and-doom scenarios in which environmental problems seem overwhelming and individuals are left powerless. On the other hand, simplistic solutions such as turning off the lights or recycling paper, while admirable in themselves, are surface level responses which are clearly not going to make a profound difference. Burdening children with the challenge of 'saving the planet' is another danger as it presents them with totally unrealistic challenges.

One way forward is to learn more about a particular issue or problem. The decline of certain iconic creatures such as tigers, whales and polar bears is a good starting point as it taps into children's natural interests and empathy for the animal kingdom. Acknowledging their fears and helping them to understand more about what is happening can be a cathartic process. Similarly, with respect to global climate change, Alexander reported how replacing unfocussed fear by factual information had the effect of empowering children (2010, p. 189). From a psychological angle, Hicks observes that when fears are brought out into the open they lose their power to haunt us (2016, p. 98). Sharing troubled feelings helps us to understand that we are not alone and contributes to our sense of agency.

Isn't this all rather negative and frightening for young children to cope with?

Sustainability education needs to be approached in a spirit of hope. It would be a travesty to think that education is about promoting a sense of despair and despondency in children. But equally it is not about cultivating bland and unrealistic optimism. Authentic hope recognizes dangers, risks and disappointments as well as opportunities, and consequently provides strength in adversity. Learning about environmental issues and the challenges that they present can be a constructive process when approached in this frame of mind. Indeed, it has the potential to be a positive force that unleashes imaginative and creative thinking – in order to create a better future we need to envision it first.

Can we learn about sustainability on a purely cognitive level or do we need to feel that it matters and engage emotionally as well?

Are we not fooling children into making them believe the world can be 'mended'?

One of the other features of sustainability education is that it addresses problems which may well be impossible to resolve. Typically, environmental issues are complex, contradictory and ambiguous and involve unexpected links and feedback loops. Bottery (2016) contrasts 'tame problems' which are definite and standardized with 'wicked problems' which are constantly changing and which have no final solution. Furthermore, he points out that 'wicked problems' are often subjective which means they can be framed in different ways. This way of thinking shifts the emphasis away from searching for solutions towards identifying questions and recognizes that knowledge is both messy and provisional.

There is a further dilemma in that environmental issues draw us into taking decisions about risks we have no way of evaluating. Climate change is a case in point. Scientists believe there are critical thresholds or tipping points for greenhouse gas emissions but they are unable to say exactly what these are and thus cannot specify safe limits. Furthermore, rising temperatures affect different parts of the globe unequally and are likely to have a disproportionate impact on people who have had no part in generating them. Future generations will be affected, too, as it takes many decades for greenhouse gasses to decay. Balancing short-term benefits with long-term consequences is a tricky process and it raises difficult moral questions. Timberlake (2009) points out that the fact we are separated from the impacts of our actions both in terms of time and space creates 'a perfect moral storm' in which we have every incentive to dissemble.

Why should we worry about the welfare of future generations, and if we do, then how far into the future does our responsibility extend?

To what extent do you think sustainability is an economic problem and nothing will change until this is realized?

Fundamentally, sustainability education challenges us to articulate our values and deeply held beliefs about what we think matters. At the moment, the dominant narrative in Western industrialized countries is centred on neo-liberalism in which the individual is king and consumption is seen as an ultimate good. Notions of development and progress are deeply embedded in this philosophy and have been enthusiastically embraced by people all over the world. However, it has now become apparent that the exploitation of natural resources can no longer be sustained at current levels. This has led to the search for different economic models centred on new ideas about wealth and well-being and underpinned by principles such as equity, community and cooperation (Rushworth, 2017; Jackson, 2017). It has also given urgency to the quest for new cultural narratives. Stibbe (2015), for example, argues that the old stories which accounted for how we came to be and relate to the world no longer make sense. The challenge of our era is to develop new myths and paradigms which will serve the needs of the future.

Transitional moments are inevitably characterized by turmoil and contradictions. This confusion is reflected in the way that sustainability is itself interpreted. According to different definitions, human beings are seen either as standing apart from nature (in a relation of stewardship) or as deeply integrated within it (as part of creation). Recognizing that we are dependent on the planet for our very existence requires a degree of humility. It also requires us to reinterpret what we mean by prosperity and wealth. This is a discussion which has yet to gain widespread social and political traction.

What do you understand by prosperity?

Many curricula are set up to ensure future generations contribute to the economic well-being of the nation. Is there room for sustainability in such driven educational systems? And even so, if only one country changes, what about the rest?

Attempting to introduce sustainability education into existing school curricula is bound to be an imperfect process. This is because the curriculum is significantly maladapted to environmental needs and priorities and focuses instead on children's future roles as workers and consumers. Reforming education to reflect an ecological world view requires a fundamentally different set of aims and values otherwise, as Orr (1992) points out, it may simply help children to become better vandals of the Earth.

The positive news is that educationalists around the world are exploring different approaches. In the UK, for example, Dunne (2016) has used over-arching concepts such as interdependence, cycles, diversity, health, geometry, beauty and oneness to focus his school curriculum on more harmonious and sustainable ways of living. Meanwhile, Assadourian (2017) cites similar examples from the United States and outlines a set of 'earthcare' principles which might inform government policy. Encouragingly, the sustainability development goals (SDGs) adopted by the United Nations (2015) now offer a framework for interactional action. For instance, SDG 4 (Quality Education) refers specifically to 'sustainable lifestyles', while some of the other goals (SDG 13, Climate Action and SDG 12, Responsible Consumption and Production) focus on the wider economic and social context.

Do you think international resolutions have any actual impact in practice?

Anticipating the future is an imperfect art but many expert commentators expect the world will change dramatically and permanently during the course of the current century. This is why Hicks gently but persuasively argues we are educating children in 'troubled times' (Hicks, 2014). Some people believe that technology will come to the rescue, though experience indicates it has failed to reduce consumption in the past. Many others are discounting the evidence of the growing environmental emergency and believe that we can continue with 'business as usual'. It seems that one promising way forward could be a shift to a low carbon and distributive economy, supported by new ways of thinking about human welfare, goals and our place in creation.

There can be little doubt that sustainability is a matter of urgency. Capra and Luisi (2014) conclude from an extensive scientific analysis that the survival of humanity in the years ahead will depend on developing a sense of ecological literacy. Orr simply states that 'time is running out on the experiment of civilisation' (2017, p. pviii). The irony is we already have many of the technologies which would enable us to live within planetary limits and that we do not need to wait for new discoveries. What we need is to agree that sustainability really is the 'elephant in the room' and to adapt our lives accordingly.

Further reading

Alexander, R. (ed.) (2010) *Children, Their World, Their Education*, London: Routledge.

Assadourian, E. (2017) 'Introduction', in E. Assadourian (ed.), *EarthEd: Rethinking Education on a Changing Planet*, London: Island Press, pp. 3–20.

Bottery, M. (2016) *Educational Leadership for a More Sustainable World*, London: Bloomsbury Academic.

Capra, F., and Luisi, L. (2014) *The Systems View of Life*, Cambridge: Cambridge University Press.

Dunne, R. (2016) 'Principles of Harmony', *Primary Geography*, 90, pp. 12–13.

Hicks, D. (2014) *Educating for Hope in Troubled Times*, London: Institute of Education Press.

Hicks, D (2016) *A Climate Change Companion*, Chepstow: Teaching4abetterworld.

Jackson, T. (2017) *Prosperity Without Growth* (2nd edn), London: Routledge.

Orr, D. (1992) 'The Problem of Education', *New Directions for Higher Education*, 77, pp. 3–8.

Orr, D. (2017) 'Foreword', in Jickling, B., and Sterling, S. (eds), *Post-Sustainablity and Environmental Education*, Cham: Palgrave MacMillan.

Rushworth, K. (2017) *Doughnut Economics*, London: Random House.

Stibbe, A. (2015) *Ecolinguistics*, London: Routledge.

Timberlake, L. (2009) *The Urgency of Now*, London: Hard Rain Project.

United Nations (2015) *Sustainable Development Goals*. Available at: http://www.un.org/sustainabledevelopment/sustainable-development-goals/ (Accessed February 2018).

28

A perspective on the perspectives

Sue Hammond

Traversing the globe in the course of this book has provided critical insights into key issues in education and offered suggestions for ways forward. It has been particularly striking that writers in ostensibly contrasting parts of the world have identified similar concerns, notwithstanding that specific contextual factors will influence how they are played out, which does seem to imply that there are common factors shaping education. Furthermore, the purpose of the book is not to offer definitive solutions but to provide questions that provoke debate. Glimmers of hope do also emerge. These are often inspired by international interactions and the realization that there are more likenesses in human behaviour than the superficial differences that divide people, and more to love about diversity than to fear.

Although travelling to another country offers a first-hand route for re-visiting one's experiences and beliefs, change can also occur through powerful vicarious experiences. The authors in this text provide vicarious experience of their professional lives and the educational lives of their students, the opportunity to peer into their settings to provoke recognition, puzzlement and perhaps shift the barriers that lead to insularity. The aim of this final chapter is to consider the future through analysing two key themes:

- Social justice and equality through education
- The impact of performativity and international comparisons

Social justice and equality through education

Equal opportunities through education is a core concern for many authors. Seeking social justice for students with disabilities, living in poverty, in war-torn countries or marginalized communities can seem a Sisyphean task. There is considerable evidence to suggest that humans are born social beings, better equipped to learn through cooperation than in isolation (Trevarthen, 2011; Tomasello et al., 2012). However, it seems there are additional imperatives to acquire social, economic, symbolic and cultural capital that advantages some social groups over others (Bourdieu, 1986). Education can be used to maintain the status quo so that those with control retain it or become the 'most powerful weapon we can use to change the world' (Mandela, 2003). An essential part of that change should be to produce equitable societies, yet educational inequalities persist in countries as diverse as Canada, England, India, Norway, Qatar, Tanzania and South Africa.

What solutions can you suggest for tackling inequality?

Among the glimmers of hope is the unified belief that educational disadvantage could be effectively served through a 'funds of knowledge' approach (Moll et al., 1992), rather than a continuation of the 'deficit ideology' (Gorski, 2016) pervading many education systems. This would require focusing on what students can do instead of what they cannot, with curricula built around their knowledge, needs and talents (as is proposed by Warrington in her discussion of UDL (in Chapter 6, Universal Design for Learning). It would, however, require dispensing with the current obsession with statistical data, international comparisons and standardization of learning.

Education practices inspired by the funds of knowledge approach start by valuing community beliefs, skills and knowledge, and considering 'diversity as a resource' (Wiltse, Chapter 7 in this text). This is a thread woven into chapters from the United States, Canada, China, Finland, Nepal and Tanzania, to name but a few. The approach creates a space in which the student is not expected to abandon or devalue their home culture, but is able to use this knowledge as the foundation for learning the linguistic and cultural practices of formal education. When students and communities feel genuinely respected, nurturing dispositions such as effortful learning, caring for each other and the environment may become realities.

Why might a 'funds of knowledge' approach have a positive effect on caring for the environment?

Even with positive attitudes and determination, there are students, nonetheless, for whom school life is a daily struggle and escape from a family cycle of deprivation seems an unattainable dream. Among the views put forward by the authors is to bring people together across countries, social or cultural groups. In order to stop demonizing the 'other', and to appreciate the importance of caring, we need to know about each other's histories, our current environmental conditions and to learn about alternative ways of living. There are several examples of projects through which global understanding is becoming a reality, including: cross-cultural student conferences, virtual visits for students, collaborative research, or teaching practicums in other countries.

A further example of the impact of cross-cultural visits are the exchanges that took place when teachers from South Korea visited schools in the southeast of England. They taught about their culture, traditions, games and language, but they also formed professional relationships with the students, sharing narratives of life in the UK and in South Korea. Such interactions have the potential for making a significant impact on those involved, challenging stereotypes, raising consciousness about cultural codes (as discussed by Olsen and Hagen), and, as Scoffham advocates, contributing to complex global understandings. The opportunity for human-to-human conversations holds the possibility for nuanced appreciation of life beyond our immediate confines as well as the effects that actions in one part of the globe can have on another. This means grappling with contentious issues, examining the realities of inequalities, human rights and morality at a time when global competition and unequal power are having catastrophic impacts.

What opportunities are there for interrogating the consequences of globalization?

Performativity, international comparisons and evidence-based practice
The amelioration of social and economic inequalities is an intended outcome of data comparisons by transnational organizations such as The Organization for Economic Co-operation and Development (OECD). Yet, for those involved in the daily 'business' of education, performativity and international comparisons have resulted in homogeneity, narrowing of curricula and pressure on students and educators. Education performance tables, accountability and standardized measures of learning have increasingly driven policy and practice in a range of national and international contexts. This issue is the most potent thread running through the book. In Part I, for instance, Findlay writes about the testing culture in

Australia, while Flognfeldt, Michaelsen and Palm discuss the prioritization of traditional, formal instruction in Norway as a result of international comparisons. In Part III, Nel and Wilson state that the best chance for inclusive practice in South Africa would be an end to politicians using school results to promote their own agendas; and McGarr draws attention to the culture in which 'successful teacher education is increasingly seen as a narrow set of pedagogical competencies rather than as a more holistic understanding of human development'.

Should education at all stages focus on holistic human development or is this impractical when countries need people with particular skill sets?

The authors who refer to the multiple impacts of accountability and assessment criteria tend towards the view that the measures have actually had an adverse effect on the quality of education. Some highlight the narrowing of the curriculum, the reintroduction of instruction methods that veer towards passivity from the students, as well as the prescriptive knowledge that is measured in both schools and in teacher education programmes. At the same time that assessments have gained authority in national education systems across the globe, their prominence in some top-performing nations or domains has been diminished. Finland, for example, has resisted the temptation to 'infect' schools with national testing because education researchers were 'unconvinced that high-stakes testing policies actually increase student learning' (Sahlberg, 2007, p. 166).

In the United States, Massachusetts gained international prestige through its results in the 2015 Programme for International Student Assessment (PISA) comparisons. Its success was ascribed to its robust accountability system and the introduction and spread of its 'charter schools'. While charter schools are required to improve their students' test results year on year, they are able to choose whether or not to follow the centrally approved curriculum, or to pay staff according to national teacher pay scales. Reforming the state's education system was intended to raise the life chances of the poorest children. Yet that same year, the Secretary of Education, Paul Reville, admitted that the performance gap between children from poor families and their wealthier counterparts persists, primarily because of the social capital enjoyed by families in financially advantaged circumstances (Reville, 2015). Likewise in Part II of this text, Hilde Tørnby writes of the capabilities of privileged students in one part of Oslo, Norway, compared to the 'troubled children' in schools in another part of the city.

In what ways might the ubiquitous testing culture be improving or exacerbating students' life chances?

The evidence that accountability and comparisons are genuinely improving the quality of education and opportunity for disadvantaged students is highly contentious. In some countries, measures seem to be detrimentally affecting the retention of teachers and the motivation of some students. There are many educationalists who challenge the reliability of tests that attempt to compare the attainment of students from incomparable family backgrounds or schooling. In England, there are multiple types of schools, ranging from private schools situated in breathtakingly beautiful historic buildings, to state schools struggling to maintain the fabric of buildings. Indeed, state funding cuts resulting in increased class sizes occurred at the same time as the UK government allocated £9.7 billion to fund new privately run 'free' schools, and to expand the selective grammar school system (DfE, 2017).

What equality benefits can selective education actually provide?

Nevertheless, reducing learning to a definitive set of evidence that encapsulates exactly how learners' learn and, therefore, how teachers should teach is 'intuitively appealing' (Biesta, 2010, p. 492). Those involved in the process of educating are committed to the best outcomes for their students, but trying to distil quintessential knowledge for success in the future is problematic. Collecting evidence of students' learning 'assumes that we can eliminate all factors, aspects and dimensions that make up the reality of education' (Biesta, 2010, p. 494). An alternative perspective is that learning is situated and requires teaching that is relational and, as Alisaari, Vigren and Heikkola remind us, needs to be responsive.

The widespread use of normative, standardized measures has also led to an increasing number of 'interventions' in schools. This is a practice that Flognfeldt, Michaelsen, and Palm have observed in Norwegian primary schools, and such interventions are delivered through formal methods, rather than being informed by knowledge of young children's learning through play. Such interventions are aimed at remedying perceived gaps in young children's knowledge, but also limit time for pursuing their own passions or experiencing broader aspects of education.

Biesta (2010, p. 495) suggests that tests generally focus on the relationship 'between actions and consequences', that is, 'transactional knowledge'. Testing on such a basis may also result in transitional knowledge. Students have learnt to perform it for a particular purpose and, despite the intensive training, the interventions, that purpose is detached from family and community lives. A student's success in acting out a discrete skill today does not guarantee the continuing retention of that knowledge. It may particularly be the case for those children and young people whose cultural backgrounds are at variance to the policy makers who design the assessments; conditions which are a feature of 'closed systems ... in a state of being isolated from their environment' (Biesta, 2010, p. 496). Yet, the knowledge that is tested is considered highly valuable, essential to the success of the generation who will be playing a role in the future of their nation. Equipping students with the same knowledge as their more advantaged peers is envisioned, in fact, as enabling greater equality.

Is it possible, or desirable, to balance the needs of the state with the needs of individuals?

Looking to the future

It is far easier in many situations to identify a problem than consider solutions. Nonetheless, throughout this book there are positive models indicating pragmatic ways forward for education. There is the example from Nepal of pre-service teachers working in the community to help bring about material change. There are diverse examples of transformative intercultural experiences and of curricula underpinned by values, sometimes explicit, at other times implicit. In Malaysia, social values are embedded in the curriculum alongside content knowledge. In Finland, nationally agreed values, such as social equality, are at the heart of education policy (Salhberg, 2007, 2015). These beliefs still encapsulate the need for students to be taught new information and skills and to be enthusiastic learners. All too often, humans adopt binary positions on prickly subjects – and education is undoubtedly such a subject – yet combining perspectives does not necessitate capitulation.

What do you consider to be universal values for education?

Considering issues through the lenses offered by international perspectives concentrates attention on what is universally important and how the ensuing principles can be achieved. Values have to be lived as well as articulated, so what values are articulated through action in the chapters? To cite a few, Chapter 18 in Part II by Collett demonstrates how 'caring for' students holistically was the core principle for an entire course. Empowering them to manage their own well-being helped the students to develop strategies for supporting their peers and to support the well-being of school students from backgrounds very different to their own. For Matthews, volunteering to teach in a refugee camp was motivated by 'caring about' the situation of displaced people but she also cared for the traumatized students. This required attuning to them, being responsive and allowing time for building trusting relationships. The teachers interviewed by Ramos-Arias continue to strive to make a difference to their students' lives. No matter how desperate the situation is in Venezuela, how little money or support is available, they care about their students' futures, providing even the poorest students with an education.

In the penultimate chapter, Scoffham provides the collective reminder that we cannot afford to stop caring about the education to which children are exposed. If our world is to survive, we have to live within planetary limits and it is imperative that students care for each other and the environment. Whether it is the desire to establish a lost status or dominance over others, whatever separates cultures and communities, the issue of sustainability is beyond national boundaries. These examples are merely a sample from across the chapters, capturing some of the values that act as the ethical foundations for the professional work of educators. The moral purposes of teaching are intertwined in the daily lives of teachers. Though the art of teaching has been compressed into various toolkits containing procedural skills and strategies in several countries, the passion and commitment to education that emerge in this book give hope for moving forward in enriching ways.

Further reading

Blaxter, L., and Hughes, C. (2000) 'Social Capital: A Critique', in Thompson J. (ed.), *Stretching the Academy: The Politics and Practice of Widening Participation in Higher Education*, Leicester: NIACE.

Biesta, G. (2010) 'Why "What Works" Still Won't Work: From Evidence-Based Education to Value-Based Education', *Studies in Philosophical Education*, 29, pp. 491–503.

Biesta, G. (2012). 'Giving Teaching Back to Education: Responding to the Disappearance of the Teacher', *Phenomenology and Practice*, 6:2, pp. 35–49.

Bourdieu, P. (1986) *Distinction: A Social Critique of the Judgement of Taste* (Translation) Richard Nice, London: Routledge and Kegan Paul.

Department for Education (DfE) (2017) *Capital Funding for Schools*. Available at: https://www.nao.org.uk/wp-content/uploads/2017/02/apital-funding-for-schools.pdf. (Accessed May 2018).

Department for Education (DfE) (2018) *Statutory Guidance. Initial Teacher Training (ITT): Criteria and Supporting Advice*. Available at: https://www.gov.uk/government/publications/initial-teacher-training-criteria/initial-teacher-training-itt-criteria-and-supporting-advice (Accessed May 2018).

Gorski, P. (2016) 'Poverty and the Ideological Imperative: A Call to Unhook from Deficit and Grit Ideology and to Strive for Structural Ideology in Teacher Education', *Journal of Education for Teaching*, 42:4, 378–386.

Guerrero, G., Leon, J., Zapata, M., Sugimaru, C., and Cueto, S. (2012) *What Works to Improve Teacher Attendance in Developing Countries: A Systematic Review*, London: EPPI-Centre, Social Science Research Unit, Institute of Education, University of London.

Mandela, N. (2003) *Lighting Your Way to a Better Future*, Speech to launch Mindset, 16 July 2003. Available at: http://www.mandela.gov.za/mandela_speeches/2003/030716_mindset.htm (Accessed May 2018).

Moll, L., Amanti, C., Neff, D., and Gonzales, N. (1992) 'Funds of Knowledge for Teaching: Using a Qualitative Approach to Connect Homes and Classrooms', *Theory into Practice*, 31:2, pp. 132–41.

OECD (2016), PISA 2015 Results (Volume I): Excellence and Equity in Education, OECD Publishing, Paris. Available at: http://dx.doi.org/10.1787/9789264266490-en https://www.oecd.org/pisa/pisa-2015-results-in-focus.pdf (Accessed April 2018).

PISA (2015) Results (Volume III) Students' Well-Being. Available at: http://www.oecd.org/pisa/publications/pisa-2015-results-volume-iii-9789264273856-en.htm (Accessed April 2018).

Reville, P. (2015) 'Why We Fail to Address the Achievement Gap', *Education Week*, 34:36 (July 7), pp. 22–3.

Sahlberg, P. (2007), 'Education Policies for Raising Student Learning: The Finnish Approach', *Journal of Education Policy*, 22:2, pp. 147–71.

Sahlberg, P. (2015) *Finnish Lessons: What Can the World Learn from Educational Change in Finland?* (2nd edn), New York: Teachers College Press.

Tomasello, M., Melis, A., Tennie, C., Wyman, E., and Herrmann, E. (2012) 'Two Key Steps in the Evolution of Human Cooperation The Interdependence Hypothesis', *Current Anthropology*, 53:6, pp. 673–92.

Trevarthen, C. (2011) 'What Young Children Give to Their Learning, Making Education Work to Sustain a Community and Its Culture', *European Early Education Research Journal*, 19:2, pp. 173–93.

Index

mentor teachers 110
metacognition 126
microteaching, benefits and drawbacks
    of 87
minority language learners 51–2
minority language students 52–3
mixed-methods study 66
moments of openness 179–80
motivation web 5
MSF. *See* Médecins Sans Frontières (MSF)
multilingualism 131
multiple means of engagement 48
music 46

NAPLAN. *See* National Assessment
    Programme Language and
    Numeracy (NAPLAN)
National Assessment Programme
    Language and Numeracy
    (NAPLAN) 32–3
National Curriculum (NC) goals 20
national education systems 198
    political agendas 1
National Institute of Education and
    Training (NIET) 171
nationalistic othering 179
natural resources 192
Nel, M. 8
neo-liberalism 192
Nepal teacher education 85–6
    benefits and drawbacks of
        microteaching 87
    group level collaboration 88–9
    organizational level collaboration 89
    personal level collaboration 87–8
    practice in 86
    social level collaboration 89–90
NIET. *See* National Institute of Education
    and Training (NIET)
non-sufficient language skills 58
Norway. *See also* child development
    beliefs in Norway

dynamic tools 80–1
education in early childhood 79
kindergarten activities 78
learning outcomes 79
learning process 79
multilingualism 81–2
primary school 78
reading skills 80
schools and kindergartens 143
screening tests 81
standardized screening 80
students 141
teachers 140
Norwegian student teachers 139–40
    qualitative date 140–1
    reconceptualize and negotiate learning
        142
    school performance 142–3
    values and cultural codes 141–2
nurseries 184, 185

Olsen, S. 132
Onditi, H. 103
open-mindedness 181
openness, moments of 179–80
Opini, B. 103
Oslo Accords of 1993 172
Oslo Metropolitan University (OsloMet)
    139, 142

Palestine 9
    classrooms 174–5
        pedagogical approach in 172–4
    curriculum change in 172–5
    education in 173–4
Palestinian Authority 172–3
Paul, L. 125–6
pedagogy 28, 184
    approach in Palestinian classrooms
        172–3
    environment 183
    personal reflection 67–8